Clustering and Its Applications in Wireless Sensor Network

SANDIP K CHAURASIYA

Copyright © <2024> <Sandip K Chaurasiya>

Made with ❤ on the Notion Press Platform

www.notionpress.com

Contents

Preface

In recent years, Wireless Sensor Networks (WSNs) have emerged as a cornerstone of modern technological innovation, facilitating real-time data collection and analysis across a myriad of applications. From environmental monitoring and smart agriculture to healthcare and industrial automation, the potential of WSNs is immense. Central to maximizing their efficiency and effectiveness is the concept of clustering—a strategy that enables better resource management, energy efficiency, and data processing within these intricate networks.

This book, titled "Clustering and its Applications in Wireless Sensor Network", aims to provide a comprehensive exploration of clustering techniques and their pivotal role in optimizing WSN performance. The opening chapters lay the foundation by introducing the fundamental concepts underlying WSNs, detailing their classification, architecture, and protocol stack, as well as the diverse applications that leverage their capabilities.

A significant portion of the discussion focuses on clustering and its various classifications, illustrating how this technique can create logical groupings of sensor nodes, improve communication efficiency, and extend network lifespan. The exploration of both heuristic and metaheuristic approaches in clustered WSNs offers insights into strategies that are pivotal in managing homogeneous and heterogeneous networks.

Furthermore, the book delves into advanced clustering methodologies, such as differential evolution-based clustering, showcasing how these techniques cater to the unique needs of different network configurations. As the book highlights the current open issues and research directions, it hopes to inspire ongoing exploration in this dynamically evolving field. The challenges faced in WSNs, including scalability, reliability, and energy consumption, present ample opportunities for creative solutions and innovations.

The book invites you to embark on this journey through the realm of clustering in Wireless Sensor Networks. Whether you are a researcher, practitioner, or student, this book equips you with valuable insights and knowledge that not only deepens your understanding but also encourages further inquiry and advances in this exciting area of study.

Sandip K Chaurasiya

Dec. 2024

Acknowledgments

To begin with, I genuinely express my gratitude to the Almighty for providing me with the strength to finish this book. I am truly thankful for His unwavering love and boundless blessings.

I want to recognize the ongoing and steadfast support of my colleagues and friends, Dr. Abhijit Kumar, Associate Professor, and Dr. Deepak Sharma, Assistant Professor - Selection Grade, from the School of Computer Science at UPES Dehradun. I am sincerely grateful to all my friends, colleagues, co-authors, and collaborators for their tremendous support and trust.

I pay tribute to my parents for all they have bestowed upon me. I am profoundly thankful to my wife for her unwavering support and encouragement. I would also like to acknowledge my children for their love and care.

Prologue

In recent times, wireless sensor networks (WSNs) tailored for specific applications have become integral to our everyday experiences. They are employed in a variety of sectors, including healthcare, military operations, industry, hospitality, environmental monitoring, emergency response, and space exploration, playing a vital role in delivering real-time data from the physical environment where close interaction is required. However, the increasing application of wireless sensor networks introduces several challenges, leading to multiple research areas focusing on energy efficiency, coverage and connectivity, load balancing, scalability, security, and reliable communication, largely due to their inherently limited resources. Among the various challenges, energy consumption stands out as the most critical. The nodes, which rely on finite power supplies, are frequently left unattended in many scenarios and cease to operate once their batteries are depleted.

To address these challenges, node clustering has emerged as a significant strategy. Clustering considers numerous parameters specific to both the network and the nodes, allowing it to be framed as an optimization issue. The literature has put forth various heuristic and metaheuristic clustering techniques. Heuristic clustering methods require an extensive exploration of the problem space, while metaheuristic methods, being independent of the problem at hand, can be applied to optimization problems across different engineering domains, including wireless sensor networks. This book aims to thoroughly examine the key facets of designing and implementing clustering-based approaches aimed at improving energy-efficient network operations. Furthermore, it addresses several unresolved challenges and potential research directions to encourage readers to explore the field in greater depth. The readers are expected to have a basic understanding of networks, communications, and fundamental electronics.

1. Introduction

Recent advancements in Micro ElectroMechanical Systems (MEMS) technology, radio communication technology, and digital electronics have made it possible to create tiny, multifunctional, low-powered, and cost-effective devices known as sensor nodes. Different types of application-specific sensor nodes, capable of sensing various parameters such as temperature, humidity, audio, and video, can be deployed to monitor the environment. These sensor nodes produce data packets based on their measurements and send them to a base station (BS), which is accessible to end users via the Internet. This interconnected system of sensor nodes is called a Wireless Sensor Network (WSN).

Within a WSN, a sensor node can function both as a data generator and a router. Architecturally, a sensor node includes four essential components: sensing, processing, transceiving, and power units. In addition to these fundamental components, a sensor node may also feature extra units like mobility, location tracking, and power supply. The sensing unit allows the node to detect environmental changes and converts analog data into digital form using an analog-to-digital converter. The processing unit manages and controls the other components and includes an onboard processor with limited computational capabilities and minimal storage. The transceiving unit transforms the information into radio signals for transmission via radio frequency (RF) waves at the sender's end, and retrieves them at the receiver's end. Lastly, the power unit is crucial as it provides the necessary energy for the operation of all other components. Within the power unit of a sensor node, there is a battery with limited capacity; since a depleted battery leads to node failure, creating energy-efficient network operations has emerged as a top challenge in WSNs. Additionally, a power supply unit, such as a solar cell, can be integrated into a sensor node to generate supplementary energy for charging the battery. Furthermore, the mobility unit or mobilizer enables the node to relocate based on specific application needs. Similarly, the location-finding unit supports applications that require the node's current location, which may involve a global positioning system (GPS) or specialized software for providing geographical positioning through distributed localization algorithms. Such networks empower administrators to monitor, respond to, and process events within a defined environment, making them suitable for various domain-specific applications (such as civil, commercial, and industrial sectors).

Fig. 1.1 demonstrates a standard wireless sensor network wherein the nodes are deployed in the sensing field to measure the surrounding. The measurements are converted into data which is forwarded to a base station after processing them a little either using a single hop forwarding strategy or using multihop. Here, single hop refers to that the nodes forward their respective data to the base station directly; whereas, multihop approach engages more than one node to forward the data of sensor node(s) to the base station. The end user may access the field data by accessing the base station either directly or via Internet.

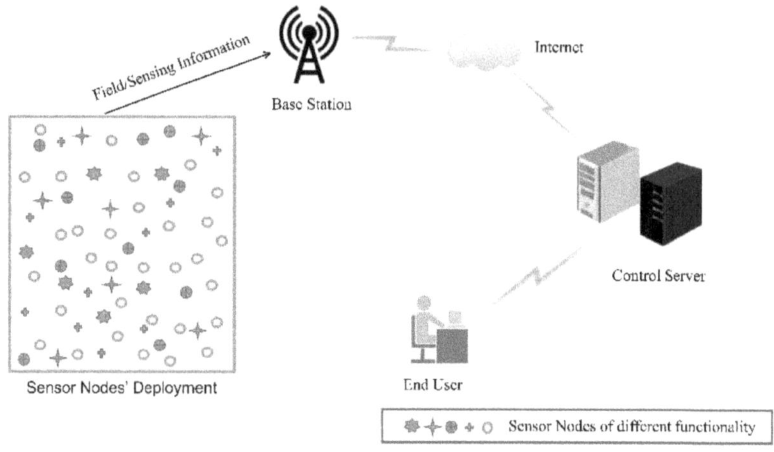

Figure 1.1 Traditional Wireless Sensor Network [1]

Classification of Wireless Sensor Network

Wireless sensor networks can be classified in various ways, such as according to the deployment environment, the diversity of nodes, their functionality, connection requirements, and mobility. Several key classifications are outlined here (Fig. 1.2):

a) Environment-Based Classification

b) Heterogeneity-Based Classification

c) Functionality-Based Classification

d) Connection-Based Classification

e) Mobility-Based Classification

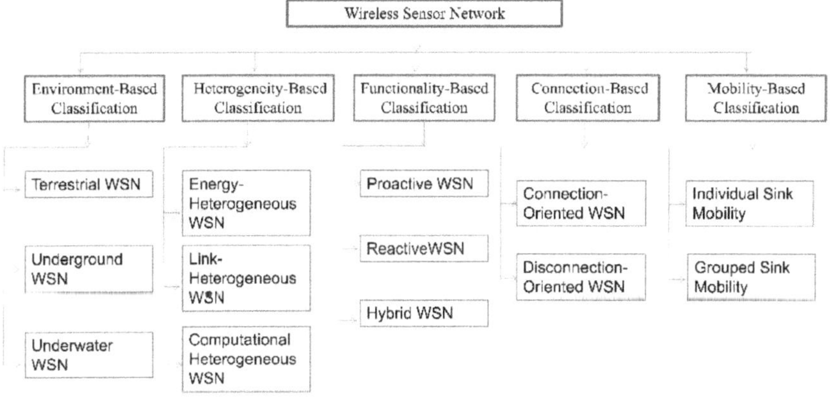

Figure 1.2 Classification of Wireless Sensor Network

a) Environment-Based Classification

Based on the environment the wireless sensor networks are developed for, WSNs can be categorized into three major classes- Terrestrial, Underwater, and Underground WSNs as follows as in Fig. 1.3:

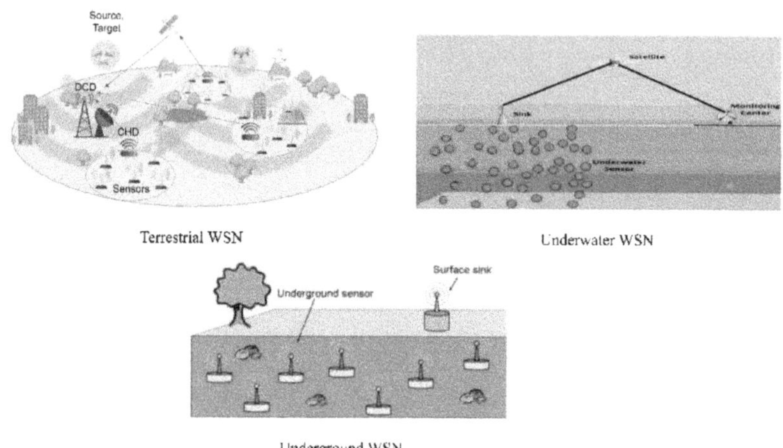

Figure 1.3 Environment-Based Classification of Wireless Sensor Network

(i) **Terrestrial WSN:** A terrestrial wireless sensor network (TWSN) consists of sensor nodes that are situated on the land or surface. A variety of sensor nodes, which have a radio frequency (RF) communication capability, can be deployed either randomly or in a planned manner. In the contexts that TWSN supports, maximizing energy efficiency is the main focus.

(ii) **Underwater WSN:** An underwater wireless sensor network (UWSN) is a network in which sensors are placed beneath the water to gather data on oceanographic conditions, monitor aquatic populations, manage disasters, and explore river environments. Within UWSN, acoustic communication is utilized instead of radio frequency (RF) communication because radio signals experience significant attenuation when transmitted through water.

(iii) **Underground Wireless Sensor Networks:** An Underground Wireless Sensor Network (UGWSN) consists of sensor nodes that are placed below the surface of the ground. Applications such as mining necessitate the use of UGWSN to assess and monitor various subterranean conditions. UGWSN can be utilized to identify the presence of minerals within mines, evaluate operational conditions, foresee potential hazardous incidents, and assist in disaster response. Similar to Underground Wireless Sensor Networks (UWSN), UGWSN cannot effectively use RF communication due to significant signal attenuation in underground settings. Therefore, it employs seismic waves or magnetic induction for communication between the sensor nodes

b) Heterogeneity-Based Classification

Due to the diversity found within wireless sensor networks, WSNs can be classified into energy heterogeneous, link heterogeneous, and computational heterogeneous categories [3].

(i) **Energy Heterogeneous Wireless Sensor Network:** Energy Heterogeneous Wireless Sensor Network (EHWSN) refers to a network where sensor nodes are deployed with varying initial energy levels. The degree of energy heterogeneity in the network can be categorized into levels, such as level-1, level-2, and so forth, based on the number of distinct initial energies present among the deployed nodes. For instance, if all the sensor nodes in the network have the same initial energy, it is classified as a level-1 or homogeneous wireless sensor network. Conversely, if the network includes nodes with two different initial energy levels, it is designated as a level-2 EHWSN. Similarly, if the network consists of sensor nodes with n different initial energy levels, it is referred to as a level-n EHWSN.

(ii) **Link Heterogeneous Wireless Sensor Network:** In the Link Heterogeneous Wireless Sensor Network (WSN), certain sensors may possess more dependable and long-distance communication links compared to others.

(iii) **Computational Heterogeneous Wireless Sensor Network:** Computational Heterogeneous Wireless Sensor Network (CHWSN) describes a network in which nodes may possess varying levels of computational capabilities. Some nodes could have more powerful processing capabilities compared to others.

Energy heterogeneity stands out as the most crucial among the three types of heterogeneities mentioned earlier. It serves as a foundation for the other two types of heterogeneity; without energy heterogeneity, link and computational heterogeneity are of no significance.

c) Functionality-Based Classification

Based on how resources are utilized, wireless sensor networks (WSNs) can be divided into proactive, reactive, and hybrid categories as detailed below:

(i) **Proactive WSN:** In a proactive wireless sensor network, sensor nodes continuously monitor the environment, generating and sending data to the base station at regular intervals. The programming of sensor nodes is designed for them to sense their surroundings at set time periods. This constant level of monitoring can lead to increased energy consumption within the network.

(ii) **Reactive WSN:** A reactive wireless sensor network features sensor nodes that are activated in response to specific events of interest. In this setup, the radio of the sensor nodes remains in sleep mode until such an event occurs. When an event takes place, it triggers the sensor nodes to relay the information to the base station. These networks are also referred to as event-driven wireless sensor networks.

(iii) **Hybrid WSN:** A hybrid wireless sensor network combines features from both previously mentioned categories—proactive and reactive WSN. It periodically senses the environment, but generally at longer intervals, while also responding to sudden changes in the network when they occur.

d) Connection-Based Classification

Wireless sensor networks can be categorized further based on their communication methods into connection-oriented and disconnection-oriented WSNs.

(i) **Connection-Oriented WSN:** In a connection-oriented WSN, it is presumed that a path between the source and the destination is always available. Two nodes are capable of communicating with each other consistently, either directly or indirectly through a multihop communication method.

(ii) **Disconnection-Oriented WSN:** In contrast to connection-oriented networks, the assumption of having a continuous path may not hold true for disconnection-oriented networks. Due to unstable communication links and unsuitable operating conditions, immediate communication between the source and destination is often not feasible. Such networks necessitate a delay-tolerant approach to data exchange. The delivery of data needs to be guaranteed within a specified delay timeframe. Examples of disconnection-oriented WSNs include UWSN, UGWSN, MWSN, and partitioned/disconnected WSNs, where issues such as sparsely deployed sensor nodes, continuous movement of nodes, and the presence of multiple disconnected network components prevent the establishment of constant connectivity among the nodes.

e) Mobility-Based Classification

Wireless sensor networks can be divided into two main types based on the mobility of nodes: Static WSN and Mobile WSN. In Static WSN, sensor nodes can alter their locations after deployment; in contrast, Mobile WSN allows sensor nodes to change their positions following the initial setup. Typically, mobile nodes are utilized either to assist static nodes or to gather data from static nodes while they are in motion. The first type of these networks is referred to as Mobile Wireless Sensor Network (MWSN), while the latter is known as Mobile Sink-based WSN (MSWSN). An MSWSN consists of at least one mobile sink tasked with collecting data from the statically deployed sensor nodes. The mobility of sinks can be categorized into individual sink mobility and grouped sink mobility.

(i) **Individual Sink Mobility:** In the individual sink mobility framework, mobile sinks navigate independently from one another to gather information from the sensor nodes. The autonomous movements of sensor nodes create three primary scenarios: controlled mobility, fixed path mobility, and random mobility models. In controlled mobility

MSWSN, the mobile sinks adhere to a guided trajectory based on certain criteria such as events of interest or the specific objectives of the application. In fixed path mobility, the mobile sinks repeatedly travel along a predetermined route. Conversely, in the random mobility model, mobile sinks follow paths that are entirely random and unpredictable to acquire data from sensor nodes. Furthermore, mobile sinks can be programmed to mimic real-world movement patterns tailored to suitable applications. There are three fundamental real-world patterns: pedestrian mobility, vehicular mobility, and dynamic mobility patterns, which correspond to the movements of walking individuals, vehicles, and entities operating in traditional environments like water and air, respectively.

(ii) **Grouped Sink Mobility**: The grouped sink mobility model features mobile sinks that operate in a cohort. They tend to stay close to one another as they navigate through the network. Each group necessitates the initial selection of a leader, around which other sinks cluster. In addition to the previously mentioned pedestrian, vehicular, and dynamic mobility patterns, grouped mobile sinks may demonstrate patterns such as regular movement, directional movement, and random movement patterns. In the regular movement pattern, mobile sinks follow a consistent route towards their destination. The directional movement pattern compels the sinks to move toward a destination, though not along specific paths. In the random movement pattern, mobile sinks traverse the network randomly.

This book mainly emphasizes on the terrestrial static connection-oriented proactive wireless sensor network

WSN Architecture and Protocol Stack

In wireless sensor networks (WSNs), sensor nodes serve the dual purpose of acting as both originators of data and routers. Therefore, communication occurs for two main purposes:

- Source function: Nodes that generate event-related information engage in communication to send their packets to the sink.
- Router function: Sensor nodes also take part in relaying packets received from other nodes to the subsequent destination in the multihop route leading to the sink.

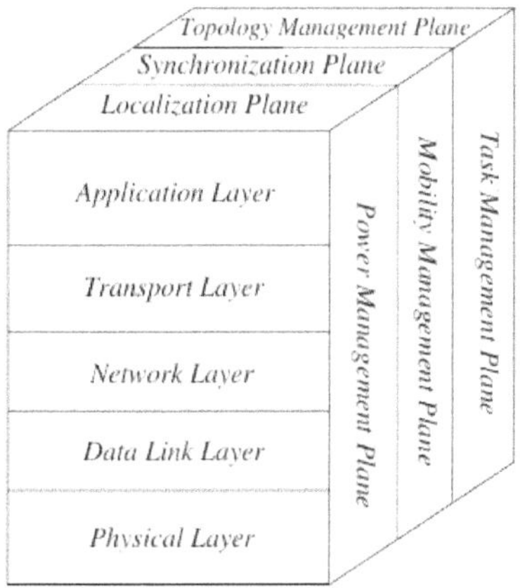

Figure 1.4 Protocol stack for Wireless Sensor Network

Figure 1.4 illustrates the protocol stack utilized by the sink and all sensor nodes [4]. This protocol stack integrates power and routing considerations, combines data with networking protocols, transmits power efficiently over the wireless medium, and encourages collaborative efforts among sensor nodes. The protocol stack comprises the physical layer, data link layer, network layer, transport layer, application layer, as well as synchronization plane, localization plane, topology management plane, power management plane, mobility management plane, and task management plane. Physical Layer focuses on robust modulation and transmission techniques in noisy environments. Link Layer ensures reliable communication and manages channel access to minimize collisions. Network Layer handles data routing from the transport layer. Transport Layer maintains the flow of data as required by the application. Application Layer supports various application software based on sensing tasks. In addition, the power, mobility, and task management planes monitor the power, movement, and task distribution among the sensor nodes. These planes help the sensor nodes coordinate the sensing task and lower the overall power consumption.

Power Management plane manages power usage, enabling nodes to turn off receivers and signal low power status. Mobility Management Plane tracks the movement of nodes to maintain routing. Task Management Plane distributes sensing tasks efficiently among nodes based on power levels, avoiding simultaneous operation. These planes facilitate collaboration among sensor nodes for efficient power usage, resource sharing, and prolonged network lifetime.

a) **Physical Layer:** The physical layer handles the selection of frequencies, the creation of carrier frequencies, the detection of signals, the modulation process, and the encryption of data. As frequency generation and signal detection are closely related to the hardware and transceiver design, they fall outside the focus of this book.

b) **Data Link Layer:** The data link layer manages the multiplexing of data streams, detects data frames, and controls access to the medium as well as errors. It guarantees dependable connections between points and from a point to multiple destinations within a communication network. More precisely, it addresses medium access and error management techniques for sensor networks.

c) **Network Layer:** Sensor nodes are densely distributed in an area, either near or within the phenomenon, as illustrated in Fig. 1.1. The data gathered regarding the phenomenon needs to be sent to the sink, which could be situated at a substantial distance from the sensor field. However, the limited communication range of the sensor nodes hinders direct interaction between each sensor node and the sink node. This necessitates the use of efficient multi-hop wireless routing protocols that connect the sensor nodes to the sink node by utilizing intermediate sensor nodes as relays. The existing routing methods that have been created for wireless ad hoc networks typically do not meet the specific needs of sensor networks.

The networking layer of sensor networks is generally structured based on the following principles:

- Ensuring energy efficiency is always a critical factor.
- Sensor networks predominantly focus on data.
- Besides routing, relay nodes can process and combine data from several neighboring nodes locally.
- Given the extensive number of nodes in a WSN, unique identifiers for each node may not be feasible, and nodes might need to be addressed according to their data or geographic location.

A significant concern for routing in Wireless Sensor Networks (WSNs) is that routing may rely on data-centric queries. Depending on the user's request, the routing protocol ought to engage different nodes that can provide the needed information. More specifically, users typically prefer to query an attribute of a phenomenon instead of inquiring about a specific node. Another crucial role of the network layer is to facilitate communication with external networks, such as other sensor networks, command and control systems, and the Internet. In one situation, sink nodes can function as gateways to different networks, while another possibility involves linking sink nodes to form a backbone that connects to external networks through a gateway.

d) **Transport Layer:** The transport layer becomes particularly important when connecting to the Internet or other external networks. TCP, due to its current transmission window techniques, fails to meet the specific challenges found in wireless sensor networks (WSNs). In contrast to protocols like TCP, the communication methods used in sensor networks do not rely on global addressing. Instead, these methods must utilize data or location-based addressing to determine where data packets should be sent. Considerations such as power usage and scalability, along with features like data-centric routing, indicate that sensor networks require a different approach in the transport layer. Therefore, these needs highlight the necessity for innovative transport layer protocols. Designing these protocols is a complex endeavor since sensor nodes face hardware limitations like restricted power and memory. Consequently, each sensor node cannot hold as much data as a server on the Internet, making acknowledgments prohibitively expensive for sensor networks. Thus, new strategies that divide end-to-end communication potentially at the sinks might be required, where UDP-type protocols could be employed in the sensor network. Within a WSN, transport layer protocols are essential for two primary functions:

(i) reliability and congestion management. Constraints on resources and high energy demands hinder end-to-end reliability.

(ii) instead of those mechanisms being used in WSNs, localized reliability strategies are essential.

Additionally, the transport layer protocols should address congestion that could arise due to increased traffic during events. Given the limitations in processing, storage, and energy use of sensor nodes, these protocols focus on leveraging the collaborative abilities of the nodes while transferring the intelligence to the sink instead of the sensor nodes.

e) **Application Layer:** The application layer comprises the primary application along with various management features. This layer contains not just the application-specific code but also functionalities for query processing and network management. A layered architecture stack was initially utilized in the development of Wireless Sensor Networks (WSNs) because of its success on the Internet. However, the extensive implementations of WSN applications show that the wireless channel significantly affects the protocols at higher layers. Furthermore, the resource limitations and the application-specific characteristics of the WSN paradigm lead to cross-layer solutions that closely integrate the layered protocol stack. By eliminating the boundaries and associated interfaces between layers, enhancements in code efficiency and reduction in operating overhead become possible. In addition to the communication capabilities within the layered structure, WSNs come equipped with various functionalities that support the proposed solutions. Each sensor device within a WSN has its own local clock for its internal processes. Every event related to the operation of the sensor device—including sensing, processing, and communication—is linked with timing information governed by this local clock. Since users seek collaborative information from multiple sensors, it is crucial for the timing information associated with data from each sensor to remain consistent. Moreover, the WSN must be capable of accurately sequencing events detected by distributed sensors to effectively represent the physical environment. These timing needs have led to the creation of time synchronization protocols in WSNs. The close relationship with physical phenomena necessitates that location information be included alongside time. WSNs are intricately related to the physical phenomena surrounding them. The information collected must be tied to the locations of the sensor nodes to provide a precise perspective of the observed sensor field.

Additionally, WSNs may track certain objects for monitoring purposes, which also necessitates the integration of location information into the tracking algorithms. Furthermore, services and communication protocols based on location require positional data. Consequently, localization protocols have been added to the communication stack. Finally, various topology management strategies are essential for sustaining the connectivity and coverage of the WSN. Topology management algorithms offer efficient methods for network deployment that lead to extended lifetimes and effective information coverage. Additionally, topology control protocols assist in determining the transmit power levels and the active duration of sensor nodes to reduce energy usage while ensuring network connectivity. Finally, clustering protocols are implemented to organize the network into clusters, enhancing scalability and extending network lifespan. The effective operation integration of each component relies on the applications running on the WSN.

The application-specific characteristics of WSNs establish several distinct features when compared to conventional networking solutions. This includes wireless sensor and actor networks, which incorporate actuators alongside sensors to transform collected data into actions that affect the environment, as well as wireless multimedia sensor networks, which facilitate multimedia traffic involving both visual and audio data in addition to scalar information. Some emerging types of WSNs, such as underwater and underground networks, present further challenges that have not been addressed by the majority of solutions designed for traditional WSNs. The qualities of flexibility, fault tolerance, high sensing accuracy, low cost, and quick deployment associated with sensor networks generate a variety of new and intriguing application areas for remote sensing. Nevertheless, the implementation of sensor networks must meet the limitations imposed by aspects such as fault tolerance, scalability, expense, hardware, changes in topology, environmental factors, and energy consumption. Given that these constraints are particularly rigorous and specific to sensor networks, innovative wireless ad hoc networking methods are essential.

Application of Wireless Sensor Network

With the progression of wireless and sensor technologies, the uses of wireless sensor technology have also broadened. Wireless sensor technology has emerged as a highly adaptable and dynamic element that has been utilized in almost all kinds of environments, including rural, urban, and suburban areas. It has fueled numerous applications. Some of these are forward-thinking, while many are practically beneficial. The variety of applications in the latter group is impressive—environmental monitoring, target tracking, monitoring of pipelines (water, oil, gas), structural health assessment, precision agriculture, healthcare, management of supply chains, observation of active volcanoes, transportation, monitoring human activities, and underground mining. Several of these are summarized in Table 1.1 and elaborated on subsequently.

TABLE 1.1 Applications of Wireless Sensor Network

Area of Application of wireless sensor network	Use
Asset Management	Monitoring of containers.

Air Traffic Control	Managing air traffic patterns.
Home Automation	Control of various home systems such as energy conservation, convenience, safety, and monitoring utility usage for electricity, water, and gas, along with home security.
Military Application	Management and reconnaissance on the battlefield, surveillance, combat field monitoring, detection of structural issues in aircraft, identification of structural defects in ships, and locating enemy vehicles.
Electricity Management	Automated meter reading, management of smart grids, and regulation of electricity load.
Biological field	Monitoring for biological agents and identification of toxic substances.
Medical	Applications for biomedicine, Smart Ambulance services, real-time patient monitoring, wireless body area networks, gathering clinical data, heartbeat sensors, and telemedicine solutions.
Road safety and management	Monitoring and managing bridges and highways.
Construction	Monitoring of buildings and structures, automation in construction, energy management in buildings, and detection of

	structural issues in construction.
Disaster Management	Detection of earthquakes, tsunami detection and response, and emergency management for disasters.
Business	E-money applications, kiosks, and monitoring and controlling workspace access with intruder detection.
Habitat	Habitat Monitoring, sensing
Industry	Monitoring and automation in industrial and building environments, manufacturing oversight, process control, inventory management, manufacturing governance, and material processing systems.
Power System	Monitoring of electrical distribution systems, implementation of smart grid sensors and networks, automated remote meter readings, thermal rating observation of conductors in power systems, and sag clearance monitoring in overhead conductors.
Transportation	Traffic monitoring, applications based on transportation, VANET-based applications, roadway management, car parking solutions, and monitoring of underground railway tunnels.

Gas Monitoring	Monitoring of sewage gas, gas pipeline oversight, gas meter tracking, and air pollution surveillance.
Other purpose	Habitat monitoring, commercial uses, consumer applications, consumer electronics and entertainment, and tracking personal belongings such as pets.

- **Sensing Seismic Events:** Seismic responses in large structures are inherently temporary and consist of frequencies below several tens of hertz. These responses can be recorded using acceleration sensors, tilt sensors, and piezoelectric sensors. However, it is essential to oversample these sensors at a high frequency to account for noise and imperfect installation. Several challenges related to data analysis include: (a) limitations concerning the characteristics of the excitations; (b) the existence of inaccessible degree-of-freedom elements; (c) noise in measurements; (d) errors in modeling; and (e) limitations imposed by the environment. The effectiveness of a method is evaluated based on its ability to extract a sufficiently large number of damage-sensitive parameters (such as stiffness and damping) from the limited and incomplete modal data obtained from an actual structure.

- **Traffic Control:** Ground transportation constitutes a crucial and intricate socioeconomic framework. Functionally, it is interconnected with and supports various systems, including supply chain management, emergency response, and public health. In metropolitan regions, this can lead to potential traffic congestion. Unfortunately, many cities around the world cannot feasibly construct new roads due to limited available space and the significant cost associated with demolishing existing streets. Many people view improved regulation of transportation systems as the sole sustainable approach to alleviating road congestion. One method of addressing traffic congestion is to implement distributed sensing systems designed to alleviate it. These systems collect data on the density, sizes, and speeds of vehicles on the roads, identify congestion, and offer drivers alternative routes and emergency exits. By utilizing video and sonar-based sensing technologies, assistance can be provided for more effective traffic management systems.

● **Health Care:** A variety of health care applications have been suggested for wireless sensor networks, such as monitoring individuals with Parkinson's Disease, epilepsy, heart issues, those recovering from a stroke or heart attack, and elderly populations. Unlike previously discussed applications, health care applications are not independent systems. Instead, they are essential components of a complex and comprehensive health and rescue infrastructure. Although many have promoted preventive health care as a way to decrease health expenses and mortality rates, research indicates that some patients perceive certain practices as inconvenient, complex, and disruptive to their daily lives. To address these challenges, research aims to deliver a clear solution that encompasses the following tasks:

- Creating pervasive systems that offer patients extensive information regarding diseases and prevention methods.
- Ensuring seamless integration of health care frameworks with emergency services and transportation systems.
- Designing dependable and unobtrusive health-monitoring devices that can be worn by patients to lessen the demands on medical staff.
- Notifying nurses and doctors when medical intervention becomes necessary.
- Minimizing inconvenient and expensive checkup appointments by establishing reliable connections between autonomous health-monitoring devices and health care facilities.

Therefore, it can be inferred from the discussion above that the wireless sensor network, which was originally intended for military uses, has now found broader applications across various sectors including medical, disaster response, business, environmental, industrial, construction, residential, and many others due to advancements in wireless and sensor technology.

Clustering and Its Classification

Wireless sensor networks inherently have limited resources, primarily due to the small size of their individual nodes. The reduced size of these nodes creates numerous constraints on the network, with the most significant being the limitation on power that must be managed. Additionally, the network consists of a vast number of nodes, which continues to increase, highlighting the need for a scalable and power-efficient framework, particularly in terms of transmission, as this has been identified as the most power-intensive activity for a node. Therefore, it can be concluded that energy efficiency and scalability are fundamental requirements for any strategy employed in wireless sensor networks.

To achieve the previously mentioned goals of energy efficiency and scalability, hierarchical architecture has been introduced, which organizes the network into multiple layers; each layer contains nodes that function similarly, meaning that nodes within the same layer perform the same tasks. In the context of wireless sensor networks, hierarchical architecture is realized through two-tier clustering, where clustering is defined as the process of grouping similar objects or identifying natural associations among them. To obtain energy efficiency and scalability, the majority of nodes are organized into several clusters at a lower level to carry out their designated tasks of sensing and transmitting the collected data to a select few nodes known as cluster heads, which handle more demanding tasks such as communication with the base station. Furthermore, this approach also helps conserve energy through data aggregation. Since the significant amount of data generated within the network is spatiotemporally correlated, data aggregation is performed by the cluster heads within their respective clusters to minimize the volume of data that needs to be transmitted, as larger data packets result in increased energy consumption during transmission. Cluster heads collect data from their cluster members, aggregate it, and then send the processed information to the base station using either a single-hop or multi-hop transmission method as required. At this stage, the end user can access the data through a suitable internet connection to apply it in their specific application. The concept of clustering is elaborated in the following Fig. 1.5.

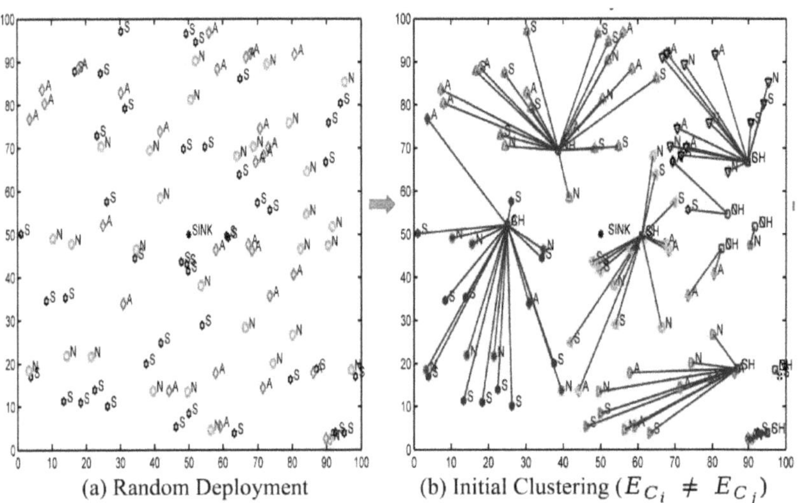

(a) Random Deployment   (b) Initial Clustering ($E_{C_i} \neq E_{C_j}$)

Figure 1.5 Clustering in a Energy Heterogeneous WSN

Figure 1.5 illustrates the organization of a 3-level energy heterogeneous wireless sensor network (HWSN) where three different types of sensor nodes are clustered together. Each cluster has an appointed node known as the cluster head (CH), selected according to a specific clustering algorithm, that coordinates activities with its cluster members to promote energy-efficient network operations.

Nodes are grouped based on shared characteristics into various clusters, and these are known as cluster members. Each cluster is represented by a designated node called the cluster head, which is responsible for collecting and processing the data received from its corresponding cluster members; the data transmitted within the clusters is termed intra-cluster traffic. Additionally, the information from the clusters is sent to the base station either through a direct method or using a multihop approach; the data exchanged between distinct clusters is referred to as inter-cluster traffic.

Given that the cluster head performs more energy-intensive tasks, such as gathering and aggregating data from its members and sending the processed information to the base station, its battery may deplete rapidly. To promote load balancing throughout the network, a rotation of cluster heads is implemented.

a) Clustering Characteristics

The clusters are entitled to some definite characteristics like cluster-specific characteristics, CH-specific characteristics, and/or procedure-specific characteristics elaborated as follows (Fig. 1.6):

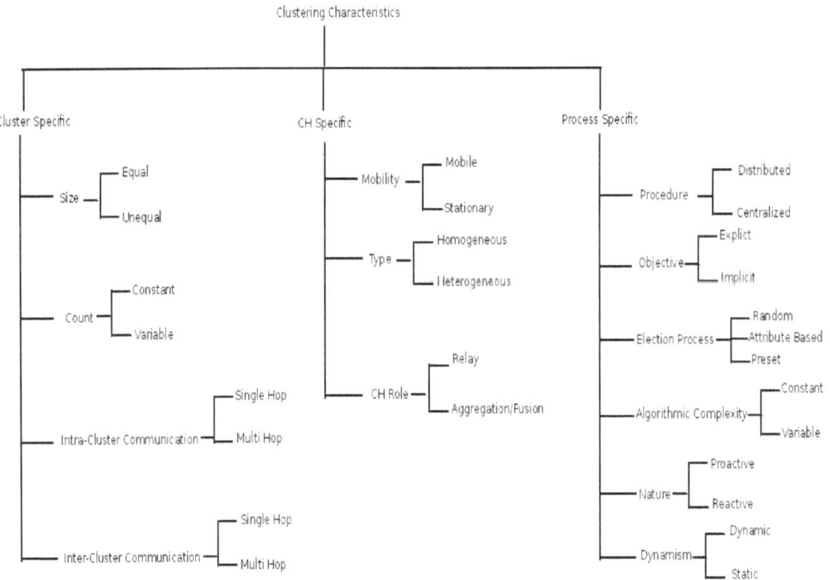

Figure 1.6 Clustering Characteristics [3]

(i) Cluster Specific Characteristics:

Characteristics that are determined based on the number of clusters formed in a network, the number of cluster members, and the communication within and between clusters are known as cluster-specific characteristics.

● Size: indicates the count of members associated with a particular cluster. The size of a cluster is influenced by the load distribution among the nodes within the network, and clusters can consist of either an equal or an unequal number of nodes after they have been established. The distance between the nodes and the base station also significantly affects the determination of cluster size.

● Count: refers to the varying number of clusters that may be established in the network over time or may remain fixed, based on the type of clustering algorithm used. In algorithms such as those proposed by [9], where cluster heads are chosen randomly in each round, the count can vary; conversely, in algorithms like those of [7], where the number of clusters is set by the base station and remains unchanged, the count is consistent.

● Intra-cluster communication: pertains to the interactions among the nodes within the cluster. Depending on the clustering approach, communication may occur through a single hop between the cluster head (CH) and its members if the cluster size is small, as the distance between the CH and its members is shorter. However, if the clustering results in larger clusters where the distance between a CH and its members is extensive, then a multihop approach may be required for intra-cluster communication.

● Inter-cluster communication: refers to the exchange of messages among the cluster heads within the network. This communication may employ a multihop strategy if there are many clusters and the distance between a cluster head and the base station exceeds the short-range communication capacity. Nevertheless, a single hop is a traditional method utilized when the distance between the cluster head and the sink remains manageable and falls within their short-range communication capabilities.

(ii) **CH Specific Characteristics:**

Given that cluster heads are responsible for the most energy-intensive tasks within the network, their attributes—including mobility, capability, and role—are essential.

● Mobility: In certain applications, cluster heads are expected to be mobile, moving within a defined range; however, managing the topology becomes significantly more complex in scenarios that require stationary cluster heads.

● Type: Depending on the network setup, nodes may be categorized as normal, advanced, or super nodes (representing homogeneous, 2-level heterogeneous, and 3-level heterogeneous networks). If the selected cluster heads possess abundant resources, they are classified as heterogeneous; conversely, they are termed homogeneous when chosen from nodes with comparable capabilities.

● CH Role: Depending on the specific needs of the application, cluster heads might either perform data aggregation/fusion or function solely as relay nodes, transmitting local traffic directly to the base station (single hop communication) or relaying through another cluster head towards the base station (multi-hop communication).

(iii) **Process Specific Characteristics**

The following characteristics are specifically related to the cluster formation process, which includes the clustering algorithm:

● Procedure: Clustering algorithms lead to procedures for forming clusters, which can be classified as either distributed or centralized. However, due to the inherently large number of nodes in wireless sensor networks, distributed methods are the most widely used.

● Objective: The objective outlines the network's purpose and can be classified as either explicit or implicit. Explicit objectives are those that the network can achieve directly, such as scalability and fault tolerance, while implicit objectives refer to indirect outcomes of the clustering process, like improved connectivity and reduced latency.

● Election Process: The processes for selecting cluster heads can be divided into three categories: preset, random, and attribute-based. As the name suggests, the preset process involves algorithms where cluster heads are predetermined prior to the deployment of nodes in the sensing area. The random process involves algorithms that select cluster heads at random, and in the attribute-based process, one or more criteria such as residual energy, distance from the base station, or associated neighbors determine the cluster heads.

● Algorithmic Complexity: This refers to the time needed for the algorithm to reach convergence. Algorithmic complexity can be classified as variable time if the algorithm's convergence depends on network specifications like the number of cluster heads, or constant time if convergence does not rely on network specifications.

● Nature: Similar to the approach taken in traditional ad hoc networks, clustering algorithms in sensor networks can also be categorized as proactive or reactive. However, there are fewer reactive networks in sensor networks compared to proactive ones, with only data-centric methods implementing the reactive type. Additionally, it has been noted that certain schemes utilize a combination of both proactive and reactive methods.

● Dynamism: Clustering dynamism is divided into two categories, dynamic and static, based on the information utilized to create clusters and select cluster heads. Dynamic schemes rely on real-time parameters, such as the current network conditions, while static schemes use predefined information for electing cluster heads and conducting other network activities, regardless of the current network state.

b) Classification of Clustering Schemes

Clustering techniques can be broadly classified into the following categories:

(i) **Dynamic and Static Clustering:** This type of categorization relates to the manner in which clusters are created. Clusters that remain unchanged over time are classified as static clustering. In contrast, if the structure of the clusters changes continuously over time, it is referred to as dynamic clustering. Additionally, there is the possibility of hybrid clustering, where the clusters may initially be dynamic for a certain number of rounds and then become static, or the reverse may occur.

(ii) **Random and Deterministic Clustering:** This classification is informed by the process of selecting cluster heads (CH). When cluster heads are selected based on a specific scheme, as seen in references [7, 8], they fall under the category of deterministic clustering schemes. Conversely, if the selection of cluster heads occurs randomly, as noted in references [9, 10], this is termed random clustering.

(iii) **Distributed and Centralized Clustering:** Distributed clustering refers to the process where clusters are formed through the collaboration of nodes. The sensor nodes share information such as their locations, residual energy levels, and degrees among themselves to determine potential clusters. In contrast, centralized clustering approaches involve a designated node, typically the base station, to facilitate the partitioning of the network.

(iv) **Equal and Unequal Clustering:** Equal and unequal clustering pertains to methods that generate clusters with either similar or varying counts of sensor nodes.

(v) **Heuristic and Metaheuristic Clustering:** Clustering schemes can be generally classified into heuristic and metaheuristic categories based on the use of intelligent strategies. Heuristic clustering, such as [7, 8, 11], requires comprehensive details about the problem, including information on nodes and networks, and follows a greedy approach. This greedy nature of heuristic methods may lead them to become trapped in local maxima or minima. Conversely, metaheuristic methods, like [12, 13], are independent of the specific problem and do not need prior knowledge of the problem details. Instead, they create optimal clusters by exploring the available search space through multiple iterations. The operation of metaheuristic schemes begins with a randomly selected set of solutions (such as initial clusters) and evolves towards forming the most optimized clusters based on the requirements of the deployed application.

In the subsequent chapters- chapter 2 & 3- of this book, the heuristic and metaheuristic classification have been dealt in the greater depth. Chapter 2 & 3 emphasize on the problem of formulating load-balanced clusters among the deployed sensor nodes. The following network model has been used in all the schemes being present in the subsequent chapters.

Network Model

- The deployed sensors have limited energy.
- All the deployed nodes are static in the sense that they are restricted from changing their locations.
- The sensors can vary their transmission power-levels.
- The sensors sense the environment on regular intervals.
- Base station is static in the sense that it never changes its location. (It can be placed anywhere in the network suiting to the nature of the application.
- The network may contain any number of nodes with any value of initial energies i.e. depending upon the intended application, the network be homogeneous or heterogeneous.

2. Heuristic Clustering in Wireless Sensor Network

As mentioned in the previous chapter, clustering involves the process of grouping sensor nodes based on shared attributes or parameters. In a clustered network structure, nodes can be categorized as either cluster heads or members. Clustering is recognized as a vital strategy for conserving network energy, particularly when data needs to be transmitted over long distances. Rather than sending their data directly to the base station, which is typically situated at a considerable distance, cluster members transmit their information solely to their corresponding cluster heads. This method of communication significantly reduces the energy consumption of the nodes, as the cost of data transmission increases dramatically with the distance between the nodes involved in communication.

Cluster formation in the network when performed heuristically requires the complete information set to search for the most viable solution and, hence, is known as a problem-dependent solution. This chapter details the clustering process through several existing heuristic solutions under various network scenarios like homogeneous/heterogeneous and static/dynamic clustering. Primarily, the schemes have been categorized as per the nodes' deployment like if all the deployed nodes have the same initial energy, it is said to be homogeneous; otherwise, heterogeneous WSN.

To illustrate how clustering has evolved as a tool for enabling energy-efficient network operations, a number of exemplary clustering-based solutions are discussed below while stating the problem and objective, narrating the approach, and discussing the outcome of adopted approach.

Heuristic Clustering in Homogeneous WSNs

This section deals with the schemes which deploy the sensor nodes with same initial energy in the sensing field for the intended application. However, the clusters may change in every subsequent network round or may remain static throughout the network lifetime. If the cluster formation takes place repeatedly during the network lifetime, the approach is referred to as dynamic clustering; otherwise, static clustering approach.

The section begins with a dynamic clustering method known as LEACH (Low Energy Adaptive Clustering Hierarchy) [9], which was the first to introduce the concept of dynamic cluster formation. Next, it discusses another well-known clustering-based approach, HEED (Hybrid Energy Efficient Distributed Clustering Approach for Wireless Sensor Network) [14], which is essentially a variation of LEACH that focuses on creating load-balanced clusters. It then moves on to a static clustering approach by providing insights into EEPSC (An Energy-Efficient Protocol with Static Clustering) [15]. Following EEPSC, the section elaborates on schemes like E^3PSC (An Enhanced Energy-Efficient Protocol with Static Clustering for WSN) [7] and EBLEC (An Energy-Balanced Lifetime Enhancing Clustering for WSN) [8], which enhance the static clustering concept introduced in EEPSC by striving for more equitable load distributions within the clusters.

a) Low Energy Adaptive Clustering Hierarchy (LEACH)

In this scheme, the authors proposed a dynamic clustering-based distributed routing method called LEACH, which requires prior knowledge of the expected ratio of nodes that will become cluster heads (CHs). It employs a randomized rotation of CHs to evenly distribute the workload among the sensor nodes and facilitates localized coordination to support scalability within the network. LEACH functions as a distributed protocol, allowing sensor nodes to independently determine their roles as CHs.

The network operation of LEACH is divided into rounds, with each round starting with an advertisement phase, followed by a cluster setup phase, and concluding with a steady-state/data transmission phase.

Advertisement Phase:

At the beginning of the clustering process, each node determines whether to act as a cluster-head for the ongoing round. This choice is influenced by the predetermined percentage of cluster heads for the network and the frequency with which the node has served as a cluster-head previously. The decision-making process involves the node n generating a random number between 0 and 1. If this number falls below a certain threshold T (n), the node will assume the role of a cluster-head for that round.

The round specific threshold T(n) is defined as follows in (1):

$$T(n) = \begin{cases} \frac{P}{1 - P * (r \bmod \frac{1}{P})} & \text{if } n \in G \\ 0 & \text{otherwise} \end{cases} \quad (1)$$

where P = the desired percentage of cluster heads, r = the current round, and G is the set of nodes that have not been cluster-heads in the last 1/P rounds. The threshold guarantees that every node will serve as a cluster-head at least once within 1/P rounds. Each node that has chosen to be a cluster-head for the current round sends out an advertisement message to the other nodes. The non-cluster-head nodes are required to keep their receivers active during this setup phase to catch the advertisements from all cluster-head nodes. Once this phase concludes, each non-cluster-head node determines which cluster it will join for this round, based on the strength of the signals received from the advertisements.

Cluster Set-Up Phase:

Once each node has determined its cluster affiliation, it needs to notify the cluster-head that it will join that cluster. Each node sends this notification back to the cluster-head utilizing a CSMA MAC protocol. Throughout this phase, all cluster-head nodes must maintain their receivers in an active state.

Steady-State Phase:

After organizing all the nodes into clusters, each cluster-head develops a schedule for the nodes within its cluster. This allows the radio components of non-cluster-head nodes to remain powered off at all times except during their designated transmission periods, which reduces energy consumption in the individual sensors. The cluster-head collects data from its members, and once it receives all the data from the nodes in its cluster, it aggregates the information and sends the compressed data to the base station. Given the considerable distance to the base station in this scenario, LEACH continuously rotates the cluster-head role in each subsequent round of the network.

From the aforementioned details of the network operation in LEACH [9], it can be learned that the scheme assumes three main characteristics like,

- Localized coordination and control for cluster set-up and operation.

- Randomized rotation of the cluster-heads and the corresponding clusters.

- Local compression to reduce global communication.

When compared with respect to the schemes like direct transmission schemes and minimum-transmission-energy (MTE) routing schemes [9], LEACH outperforms in terms of network energy dissipation (defined as total network energy consumption) and network lifetime (defined as the time when last node dies in the network) as shown in the following Fig. 2.1.

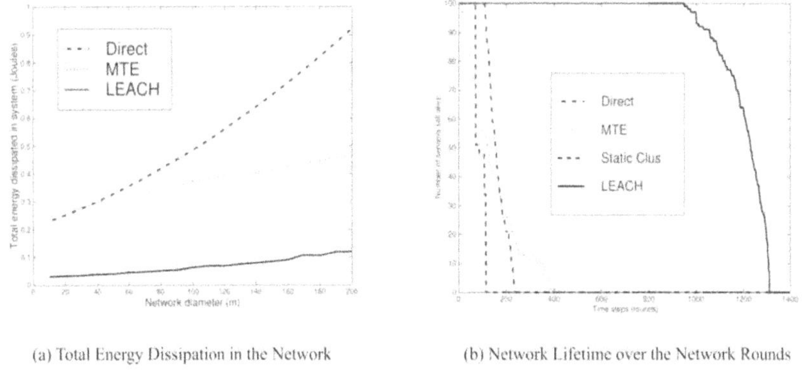

(a) Total Energy Dissipation in the Network

(b) Network Lifetime over the Network Rounds

Figure 2.1 Performance of LEACH [9]

However, because of the probabilistic decision on the role of cluster heads, LEACH fails to assure about the structure and count of the clusters in the network as demonstrated in Fig. 2.2 below.

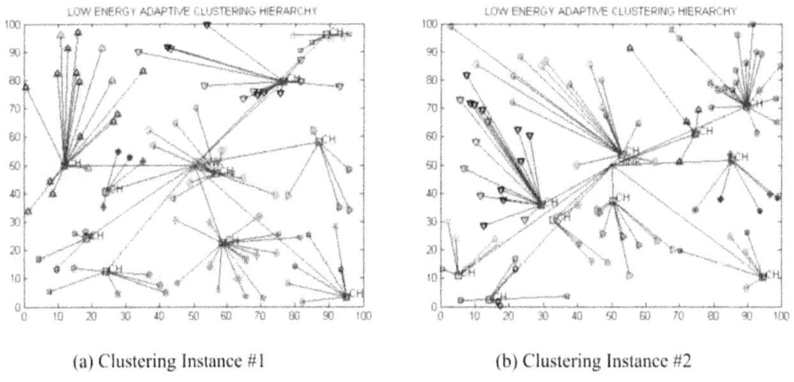

(a) Clustering Instance #1

(b) Clustering Instance #2

Figure 2.2 Cluster Formation in LEACH

Fig. 2.2 demonstrates the two clustering instances wherein it becomes obvious that LEACH doesn't assure either about cluster-count or about the cluster-strength.

b) Hybrid Energy Efficient Distributed Clustering Approach for Wireless Sensor Network

To tackle the issue of forming load-balanced clusters, HEED (Hybrid Energy Efficient Distributed Clustering Approach for Wireless Sensor Network) introduces a method that periodically chooses cluster heads based on a combination of the remaining energy of the nodes and a secondary factor, like the proximity of nodes to their neighbors or their node degree. Initially, a group of cluster heads is selected mainly based on the residual energy of the nodes. Subsequently, the degree of the nodes helps resolve any ties and facilitates the creation of evenly distributed clusters with balanced loads. HEED ensures that the clusters formed within the network remain load-balanced. While LEACH utilizes single-hop communication, HEED employs multi-hop communication to conserve energy within the network.

HEED essentially builds upon LEACH, and similarly to LEACH, the network's operation in HEED is divided into rounds. The clustering procedure at each node involves several iterations, known as Niter. Each iteration takes a duration of tc, which must be sufficient to receive messages from any neighbor within the cluster's range. An initial percentage of cluster heads out of all n nodes is established, referred to as Cprob (for example, 5%), assuming that a precise optimal percentage cannot be determined beforehand. Cprob is solely used to constrain the initial announcements of cluster heads, and it does not directly influence the final clusters. Before a node starts executing HEED, it sets its probability of becoming a cluster head, CHprob, as per the following (2):

$$CH_{prob} = C_{prob} \; x \; \frac{E_{residual}}{E_{max}} \tag{2}$$

where $E_{residual}$ is the estimated current residual energy in the node, and Emax is a reference maximum energy (corresponding to a fully charged battery). During any iteration i, $i \leq N_{iter}$, every "uncovered" node elects to become a cluster head with probability CH$_{prob}$.

After step i, the set of tentative cluster heads, TCH, is figured out and a node selects its cluster head to be the node with the lowest cost in TCH.

HEED outperforms the schemes like direct transmission and LEACH with respect to the network lifetime (defined here as the time when the first or last node dies in the network) as shown in the Fig. 2.3.

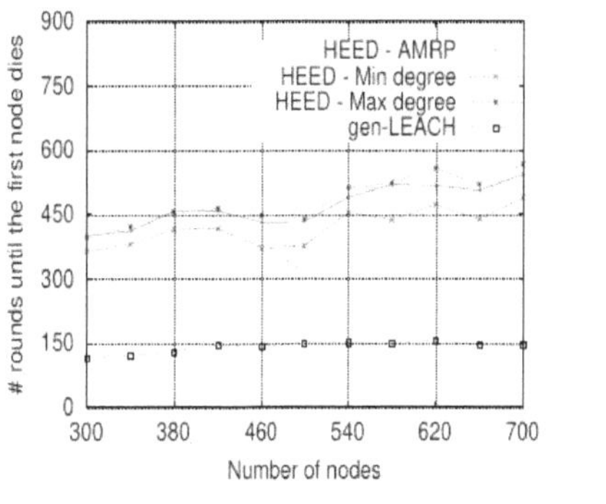

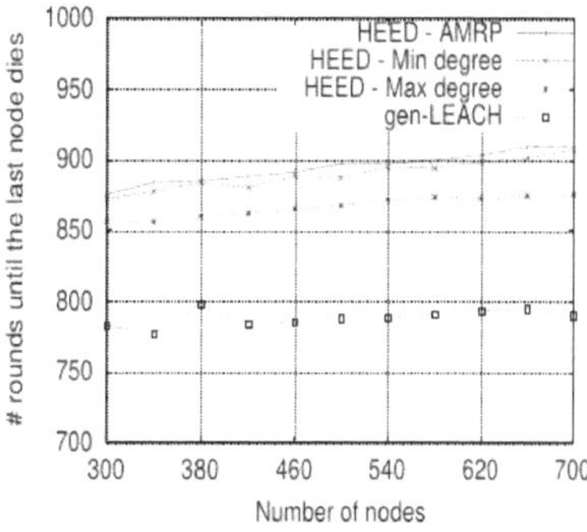

(a) Network lifetime (first node death)   (b) Network lifetime (last node death)

Figure 2.3 Performance of HEED [14]

c) An Energy-Efficient Protocol with Static Clustering

The above-discussed schemes (LEACH and HEED) are the dynamic clustering schemes which provision dynamic clusters' formation in the subsequent rounds. Such clustering strategies impose an additional clustering overhead lowering the effective network lifetime. To eliminate this requirement of repeated cluster-formation in every network round, EEPSC was introduced with the notion of distance-based static clustering wherein, clusters once formed remain static throughout the network lifetime. EEPSC evenly distributes the network load among the sensor nodes through the concept of temporary cluster heads (TCHs). EEPSC supersedes LEACH with respect to network lifetime. It starts the network operation with the distance-based clusters' formation. Immediately after the distance-based network partitioning, EEPSC selects the appropriate nodes for the role of cluster heads based on nodes' residual energy.

EEPSC select a node with the maximum remaining energy in the cluster as CH, and that with the minimum residual energy as temporary CH. Then, data transfer between the nodes and the BS takes place.

The detail of the scheme is as follows:

Like LEACH and HEED, the network operation of EEPSC is also broken into rounds where each round consists of three phases- setup, responsible node selection, and steady-state phases.

Setup Phase:

During this stage, the base station transmits (k-1) unique messages with varying transmission powers, where k represents the desired number of clusters. When sensor nodes receive the broadcast for $k=j$ (with j being less than k), they assign their cluster ID as j and notify the base station of their membership in cluster#j through a JOIN-REQ message. Subsequently, any sensor nodes that have not joined a cluster assign their cluster ID to k and inform the base station.

Following this, the base station randomly chooses a temporary cluster head (CH) for each cluster and disseminates the cluster information throughout the entire network. The base station also creates a TDMA schedule for the nodes and sends it to the nodes within each cluster.

Responsible Node Selection Phase:

At the start of each round, every node in the cluster transmits its energy level to the temporary-CH during its designated time-slot. Subsequently, the temporary-CH selects the sensor node with the highest energy level as the CH for the ongoing round; meanwhile, the node with the lowest energy level is designated as the temporary-CH for the subsequent round and sends a round-start packet that includes the ID of the new responsible sensor for the current round. This packet also signifies the commencement of the round to the other nodes.

Steady-State Phase:

The steady-state phase is segmented into frames where nodes transmit their data to the Cluster Head (CH) during designated time slots. The transmitted data includes the node ID and the parameters that have been sensed. In this method, a Direct Transmission approach is used for the communication between the CH and the base station. Each slot duration for data transmission remains constant, meaning the time required to send a frame varies based on the total number of nodes within the cluster. To minimize energy consumption, each non-cluster head node has its radio turned off until it's time for its designated transmission, while the CHs need to stay awake to collect all the data from the cluster's nodes.

As a matter of fact, EEPSC outperforms LEACH in terms of various network parameters like network lifetime, throughput, and network energy consumption etc. as shown in the self-explanatory figure- Fig. 2.4.

While EEPSC [15] generally provides better performance than LEACH [9], selecting nodes that are closer to the boundary as cluster heads can sometimes lead to increased communication costs for nodes on the opposite side of the boundary, potentially causing quicker battery depletion in those nodes.

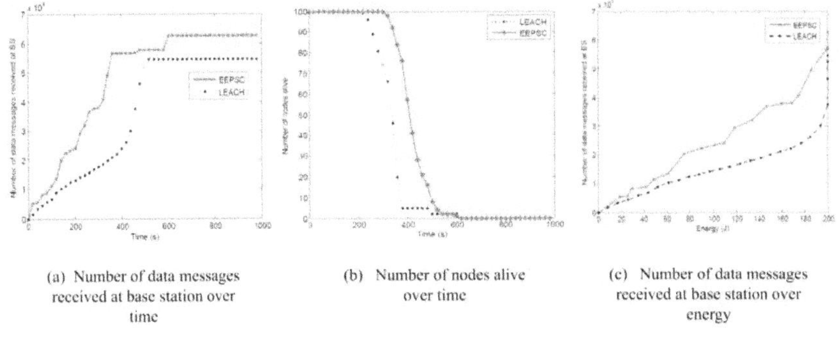

(a) Number of data messages received at base station over time

(b) Number of nodes alive over time

(c) Number of data messages received at base station over energy

Figure 2.4 Performance of EEPSC [15]

d) An Enhanced Energy-Efficient Protocol with Static Clustering (E³PSC) for WSN

In EEPSC, the selection of cluster-heads is conducted based on the remaining energy levels of the nodes, and a temporary cluster-head is utilized during the selection process. The node that has the highest remaining energy within a cluster is chosen as the cluster-head for that round. If this newly appointed cluster-head is situated near the boundary of the cluster, the energy usage for other member nodes in the cluster may rise as they transmit the collected data to the cluster-head. Consequently, frequently selecting nodes positioned closer to the boundary as cluster-heads can elevate the communication costs for nodes situated on the opposite side of the boundary, which could lead to a faster depletion of the batteries on those nodes. Therefore, the spatial arrangement of nodes within the cluster is a crucial factor, and it should be taken into account during the cluster-head selection process.

E^3PSC [7] addresses the shortcomings of EEPSC by choosing a cluster-head located as centrally as possible within a cluster, thereby reducing energy consumption during intra-cluster communication (from member nodes to the cluster-head). Similar to EEPSC [15], E^3PSC is also a self-organizing, static clustering method where clusters are established just once throughout the entire network operation. The overall operation of the network consists of multiple rounds, with each round further divided into three distinct phases: the setup phase, the responsible node selection phase, and the steady-state phase.

The detail of the scheme is as follows:

Setup Phase:

This phase resembles the EEPSC approach [15]. Clusters are established only once at the beginning of the network's operation. The base station transmits (k - 1) successive messages at varying transmission powers, with k representing the desired number of clusters determined by the sink. Nodes that receive these successive messages, indexed as i = 1, 2, 3, ..., (k-1), assign themselves a cluster-id of i and notify the base station of their intention to join the cluster through a JOIN-REQ message. Finally, nodes that did not receive any messages set their cluster-id to k and inform the base station with a JOIN-REQ message. Sensor nodes utilize CSMA to avoid collisions while sending the JOIN-REQ messages to the base station. Following the formation of clusters, the base station calculates the mean positions of the node distribution within each cluster. Subsequently, the base station determines the distance of all nodes from the mean positions within their respective clusters. Additionally, the base station randomly chooses a temporary cluster-head (TCH) for each cluster and develops a TDMA schedule for the nodes within every cluster of the network. After performing all these executions, base station transmits above computed details i.e. TCH, TDMA-schedule, and nodes' distance from their respective clusters' mean position (i.e. $d_{mean}{}_i^{\,j}$) to the nodes. Once all the nodes receive the 3-tuple data, set-up phase is complete.

Responsible Node Selection Phase:

In this phase, cluster-heads (CHs) for the current round and the temporary-cluster-heads (TCHs) for the next round are selected in each cluster. In this phase at the beginning of every round, nodes in each cluster send 2-tuple data $(E_{residual}{}_i^{\,j}, d_{mean}{}_i^{\,j})$ to the corresponding TCH. TCH then declares the node with the highest value of ($\frac{E_{residual}}{d_{mean}}$) as cluster head for the current round; Node with the second highest value of$(\frac{E_{residual}}{d_{mean}})$ is selected as TCH for next round. Then CHs broadcast a round-start packet including responsible nodes' id into their respective clusters indicating beginning of round to other sensor nodes.

Steady-State Phase:

This stage is identical to the steady-state phase of EEPSC [15]. During the steady-state phase, nodes transmit the collected data to their respective Cluster Heads (CHs) within their assigned time slots, which leads to a structure where the phase is further divided into frames. As the length of each time slot is constant and fixed, the time taken to transmit a frame relies on the number of nodes within the clusters. A direct transmission method is employed for communication between CHs and the base station. In each cluster, the radios of the member nodes remain off until their designated time slot, while the radio of the cluster head is always active to receive data from all the nodes.

E^3PSC outperforms EEPSC in terms of network lifetime, throughput, and energy consumption as evident from Fig. 2.6.

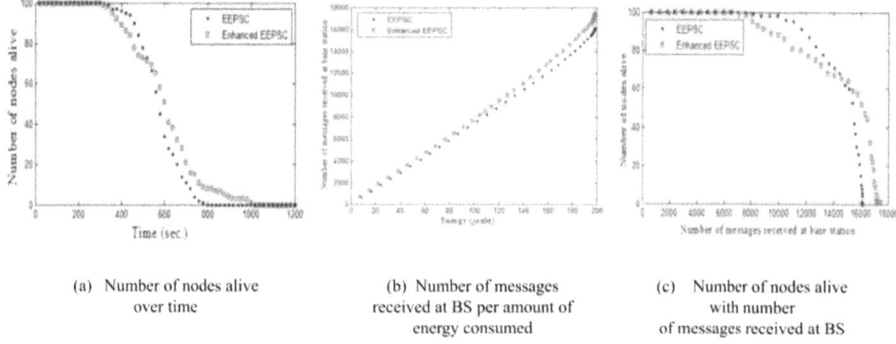

<table>
<tr><td>(a) Number of nodes alive
over time</td><td>(b) Number of messages
received at BS per amount of
energy consumed</td><td>(c) Number of nodes alive
with number
of messages received at BS</td></tr>
</table>

Figure 2.6 Performance of E^3PSC [7]

The above-mentioned schemes are the examples how clustering can be implemented objectively for homogeneous wireless sensor network. Following sections detail the implementation of clustering in heterogeneous wireless sensor network.

Heuristic Clustering in Heterogeneous WSNs

Similar to its predecessor, this section begins with the dynamic clustering approach, EDDEEC [16], designed for heterogeneous wireless sensor networks (HWSN) featuring three levels of energy heterogeneity, where the network is composed of three categories of nodes: super, advanced, and normal nodes. It then outlines a static method, HEECP [17], which facilitates energy-efficient operations in a 3-level HWSN. The section concludes with a hybrid clustering strategy, EEHCT [18], which initiates with a LEACH-like dynamic clustering technique but stabilizes the clusters once the most optimal set of load-balanced clusters is identified. The clusters established will remain unchanged for the entire duration of the network's lifespan. Additionally, prior to exploring the aforementioned schemes, the concept of 3-level energy heterogeneity is provided here for the readers' understanding as follows:

In the 3-level HWSN, there are three categories of nodes: normal, advanced, and super nodes that are distributed across the sensing area. Each type of node has a different initial energy level, such that E_{super} is greater than $E_{advanced}$, which in turn is greater than E_{normal}; E_{super}, $E_{advanced}$, and E_{normal} correspond to the initial energies of the super, advanced, and normal nodes respectively. The nodes are placed in different proportions, meaning that if N is the total number of nodes deployed and m represents the fraction of non-normal nodes, then m.N nodes will consist of advanced and super nodes, leaving $(1 - m.N)$ nodes as normal nodes.

Additionally, if m_0 indicates the fraction of super nodes, it can be straightforwardly calculated that there will be $m.m_0.N$ super nodes and $(1-m.m_0.N)$ advanced nodes in the network. Furthermore, if the initial energy of the normal nodes is denoted as E_0, then the initial energies of the advanced and super nodes will be $E0 + a.E_0$ and $E_0 + b.E_0$ respectively, where a and b are the energy multipliers established by the network administrator.

a) Enhanced Developed Distributed Energy-Efficient Clustering (EDDEEC) for Heterogeneous Wireless Sensor Networks

Similar to LEACH, EDDEEC [16] utilizes a probability-based method for selecting cluster heads. In this selection process, EDDEEC needs parameters such as the remaining energy of nodes and the average energy within the network. When the remaining energy of the non-regular nodes falls below a specific threshold, all three types of nodes are considered equally for choosing the cluster head. The specifics of the approach are as follows:

The operation of the network is divided into rounds, with each round starting with an advertisement phase, followed by a cluster set-up phase, and finishing with a steady-state/data transmission phase, similar to LEACH.

Advertisement Phase:

In a manner similar to LEACH, each node determines whether to act as a cluster-head for the ongoing round based on a predetermined percentage, popt, of cluster heads for the network and the number of times the node has served as a cluster-head, represented as G. Node n makes this decision by generating a random number between 0 and 1. If this number falls below a certain threshold T(n), the node will serve as a cluster-head for the current round. The round specific threshold T(n) is defined as in (2), i.e.

$$T(n) = \begin{cases} \dfrac{p_i}{1 - p_i(r \bmod \frac{1}{p_i})}, & \text{if } n \in G \\ 0, & \text{otherwise} \end{cases} \qquad (3)$$

where,

$$p_i = \begin{cases} \dfrac{p_{opt}E_i(r)}{(1+m(a+m_0b))\bar{E}(r)}, & \text{if node is a normal node and } E_i(r) > T_{absolute} \\ \dfrac{p_{opt}(1+a)E_i(r)}{(1+m(a+m_0b))\bar{E}(r)}, & \text{if node is an advanced node and } E_i(r) > T_{absolute} \\ \dfrac{p_{opt}(1+b)E_i(r)}{(1+m(a+m_0b))\bar{E}(r)}, & \text{if node is a super node and } E_i(r) > T_{absolute} \end{cases}$$

$$(4)$$

Here, m is the fraction of non-normal nodes; m_0 is the fraction of super nodes; $E_i(r)$ is the residual energy of the ith node in rth round.

$\bar{E}(r)$ can be defined as follows:

$$\bar{E}(r) = \frac{1}{N} E_{total}\left(1 - \frac{r}{R}\right) \qquad (5)$$

$$R = \frac{E_{total}}{E_{round}} \qquad (6)$$

$T_{absolute}$ is experimentally configured to $(0.7)E_0$, at which point all normal, advance, and super nodes share the same chances of being selected as cluster heads, and instead of (3), (1) is utilized for the purpose of CH selection. Each node that has designated itself as a cluster head for the ongoing round sends out an advertisement message to the remaining nodes. Non-cluster-head nodes must keep their receivers active during this setup phase to catch the advertisements from all cluster-head nodes. Once this phase concludes, each non-cluster-head node determines which cluster it will join for this round based on the strength of the received advertisement signal.

Cluster Set-Up Phase:

Similar to LEACH, after each node determines its cluster affiliation, it is necessary for it to notify the cluster-head that it intends to become a member of the cluster. Each node sends this information back to the cluster-head utilizing a CSMA MAC protocol. Throughout this phase, all cluster-head nodes are required to keep their receivers active.

Steady-State Phase:

This phase closely resembles the LEACH protocol [9], too. EDDEEC shows superior performance compared to several methods, such as DEEC [19], DDEEC [20], and EDEEC [21], in terms of network lifetime and throughput, as illustrated in Fig. 2.7. Nevertheless, the primary drawbacks of this approach are the recurring formation of clusters in each subsequent round and the dependency on energy heterogeneity.

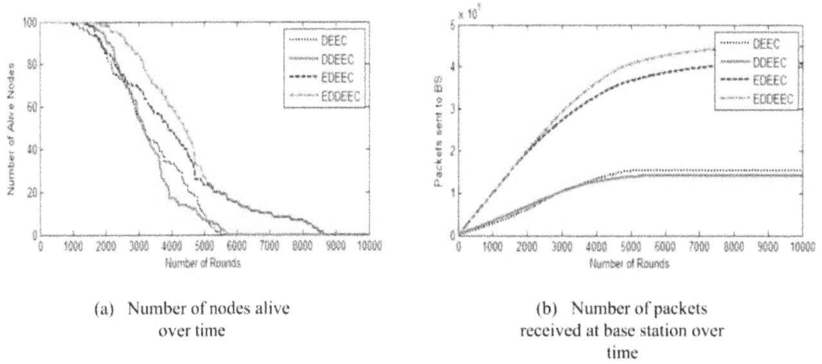

(a) Number of nodes alive over time

(b) Number of packets received at base station over time

Figure 2.7 Performance of EDDEEC [16]

b) Heterogeneous Energy-Efficient Clustering Protocol (HEECP) for Wireless Sensor Networks

To address the previously mentioned shortcomings of the EDDEEC, a static clustering approach was introduced for 3-level HWSN, known as the Heterogeneous Energy-Efficient Clustering Protocol (HEECP) for Wireless Sensor Networks. HEECP tackles energy heterogeneity by deploying nodes with varying initial energy levels within the network. It operates under the assumption of a 3-level HWSN, wherein nodes can possess one of three different initial energy levels throughout the duration of the network's function. Nevertheless, it is capable of accommodating any degree of energy heterogeneity present in the network. Similar to E^3PSC, HEECP initiates its process by segmenting the network into a limited number of distance-based clusters. Once this fixed distance-based clustering is established for the entire network lifetime, HEECP identifies the centers of cluster energy (CoCE) for each cluster. After determining the CoCEs for every cluster, cluster heads are selected in proximity to those centers to minimize energy expenditure for member nodes during intracluster communication. Subsequently, data transmission takes place, enabling the relay of cluster data to the base station. The specifics of the scheme are outlined as follows:

As seen in E^3PSC, HEECP organizes the network operation into rounds. Within each round, there are distinct phases: setup, responsible node selection, and steady state. The setup phase occurs only once to establish BS-supported distance-based clusters, after which the responsible node selection and steady-state phases are repeated in every following round.

Setup Phase:

Similar to its previous scheme [7], HEECP begins its network operation by creating distance-based clusters initiated by the base station (BS). To do this, the BS transmits $k - 1$ signals, each at different power levels. Upon receiving the ith (where $i \in [1, k - 1]$) broadcast, the sensor nodes express their intent to join the ith cluster by sending JOIN-REQ messages. After the final broadcast from the BS, any nodes that have not joined a cluster will automatically be assigned to the kth cluster. Once the base station has established the clusters, it assigns a time division multiple access (TDMA) schedule for each cluster. The BS also randomly selects a node for each cluster to act as the temporary cluster head (TCH) and communicates the pair (*TDMA$_i$, TCH$_i$*) to the ith cluster. A TCH is a designated node selected by the base station, primarily tasked with overseeing the selection of cluster heads (CHs) within its specific cluster.

Responsible Node Selection Phase:

Following the establishment of distance-based clusters within the network, the next phase involves selecting responsible nodes for execution. During this phase, Cluster Heads (CHs) are chosen for the current round, while Temporary Cluster Heads (TCHs) are designated for the upcoming rounds within each cluster. In cluster i, the member nodes communicate their specific details, such as location and energy status, to their assigned TCHi during the designated TDMA slots.

On the basis of information received from the nodes, TCHi locates the center of cluster energy (CoCE) as per the following (7):

$$(X_{CoCE_i}, Y_{CoCE_i}) = \left(\frac{\sum_{j=1}^{l} x_i^j * ResE_i^j}{\sum_{j=1}^{m} ResE_i^j}, \frac{\sum_{j=1}^{l} y_i^j * ResE_i^j}{\sum_{j=1}^{m} ResE_i^j}\right) \tag{7}$$

where, l is length of the ith cluster and $ResE_i^j$ is the jth sensor node's remaining energy in ith cluster. Once the CoCEs are determined for each cluster, the nodes closest to these points are selected as the cluster heads in their respective clusters for the ongoing network round, and the nodes with the least amount of residual energy are selected as TCHs for the next round. TCHs then broadcast this pair of information to their respective cluster members.

Steady State Phase:

In a traditional steady state phase, the members of the cluster send their sensor readings to their designated cluster head during the assigned time slots. The cluster heads then consolidate the data and relay it to the base station for access by the end-users. HEECP shows significantly better performance compared to EEPSC and E³PSC in managing 3-level energy heterogeneity, as illustrated in Fig. 2.8, particularly regarding network lifetime and energy consumption.

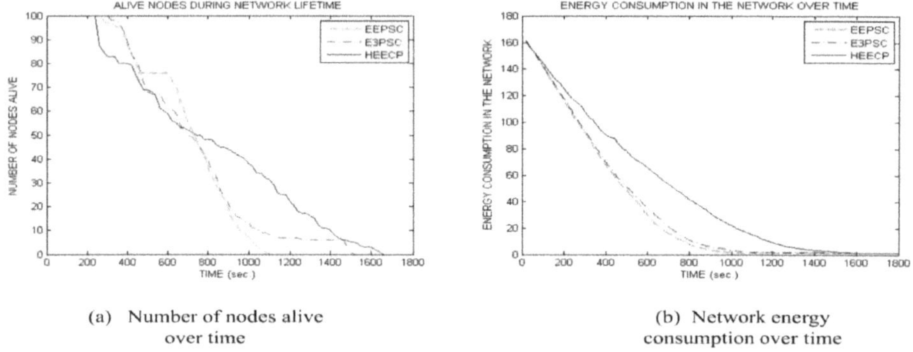

(a)   Number of nodes alive
over time

(b)   Network energy
consumption over time

Figure 2.8 Performance of HEECP [17]

c) Energy-Efficient Hybrid Clustering Technique (EEHCT)

EEHCT [18] addresses the n-level energy heterogeneity within the network and effectively combines both dynamic and static clustering methods. An n-level HWSN represents a wireless sensor network that includes n varieties of sensor nodes, which may vary in capability, functionality, or energy levels. Similar to the previously mentioned scheme, EEHCT focuses on energy heterogeneity, where the network can consist of nodes with n distinct levels of initial energy.

As a network solution based on clustering, EEHCT initially divides the network into a finite set of clusters. Following that, it manages the selection of cluster heads and initiates the data transmission process within the network. For the cluster partitioning process, EEHCT utilizes a hybrid clustering approach. A hybrid clustering approach combines both static and dynamic clustering methods, leveraging the advantages of each traditional clustering method to achieve load-balanced cluster formation. Dynamic clustering faces the significant drawback of incurring repeated costs for cluster formation in each round. On the other hand, static clustering is challenged by the creation of

44

unbalanced clusters, which can severely impact the network's lifetime since clusters cannot be modified once established. Consequently, EEHCT smartly integrates both strategies (thus employing hybrid clustering) to promote load-balanced network partitioning. It begins with dynamic clustering while monitoring the clusters being established in the network. Once it identifies a load-balanced clustering scenario, it solidifies that arrangement for the remainder of the network's lifetime. Afterward, by rotating the role of cluster heads among the appropriate sensor nodes, EEHCT effectively continues with other network functions as needed. The scheme's details are as follows:

Similar to its predecessors [7-17], EEHCT organizes the network operations into rounds. Each round consists of two stages: the setup phase and the steady-state phase. During the setup phase, EEHCT divides the network into a limited number of clusters, while the steady-state phase manages the data transfer.

Setup Phase:

The setup phase consists of two subphases: dynamic and static. The process commences with the dynamic subphase and transitions to the static one depending on the beacon messages indicating static=FALSE and static=TRUE from the base station. At the onset of network operations, the base station sends out a beacon with static=FALSE, prompting the nodes to carry out the standard Received Signal Strength Indicator (RSSI)-based dynamic clustering as referenced in [9]. However, once the base station detects that energy-balanced clusters are formed based on the input from the Cluster Heads (CHs), it promptly broadcasts another beacon with static=TRUE to solidify the current network partitioning for the duration of the network's lifespan.

Steady State Phase:

Similar to the conventional steady-state phase, the member nodes within a cluster relay their sensing information to their designated cluster head during the assigned TDMA slots. The cluster head then compiles and transmits the gathered data to the base station. However, EEHCT requires each cluster head to provide additional details regarding the average residual energy of its cluster, referred to as ACE. The base station utilizes this information to assess the creation of energy-balanced clusters. The base station compares the average energy levels of the clusters. When the base station identifies clusters with comparable energy levels, it promptly broadcasts a beacon with static=TRUE to the network, indicating that no further modifications to the clusters will be considered. Alongside this beacon broadcast, the cluster heads in the current cluster formation are designated as temporary cluster heads (TCHs) for their respective cluster members. The primary role of the temporary cluster heads is to aid in the selection of cluster heads in the upcoming rounds. Fig. 2.9 depicts the entire functioning of the EECHT scheme as follows:

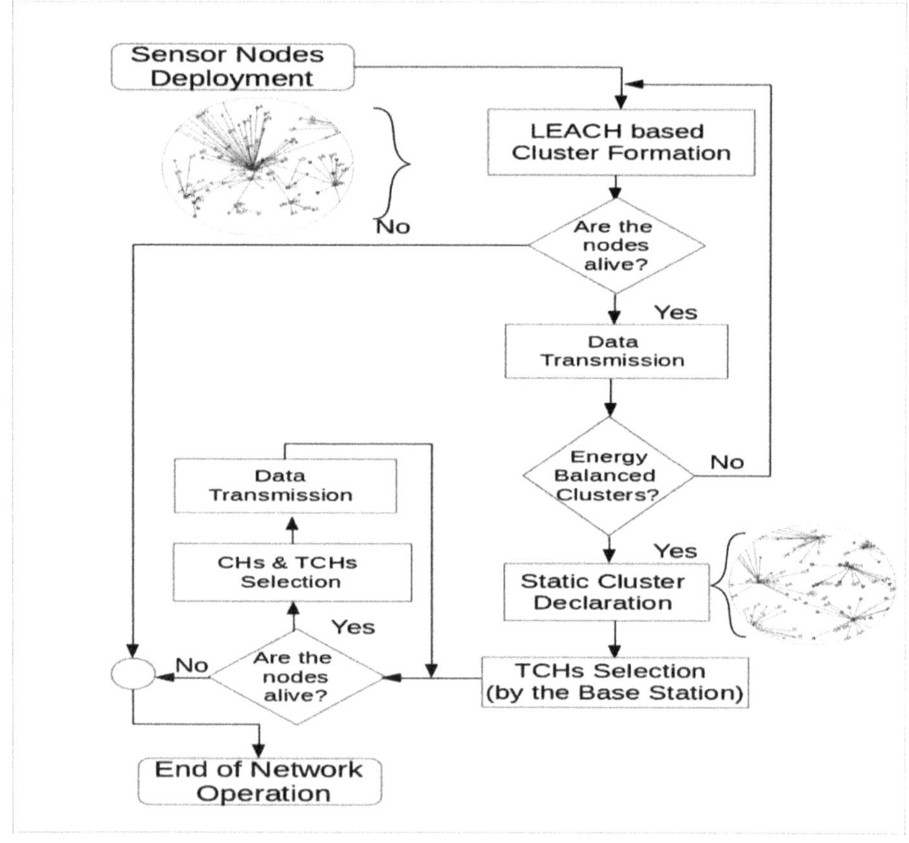

Figure 2.9 Working of EEHCT [18]

EEHCT outperforms its contemporary counterparts like [9, 19-24] in terms of network lifetime, throughput, formation of load-balanced clusters, and network energy consumption as demonstrated in self-explanatory Fig. 2.10, 2.11, and 2.12. Meanwhile, the authors have also demonstrated the efficacy of their scheme under varying network parameters like with varying proportion of normal, advanced, and super nodes (as in 3-level energy heterogeneity).

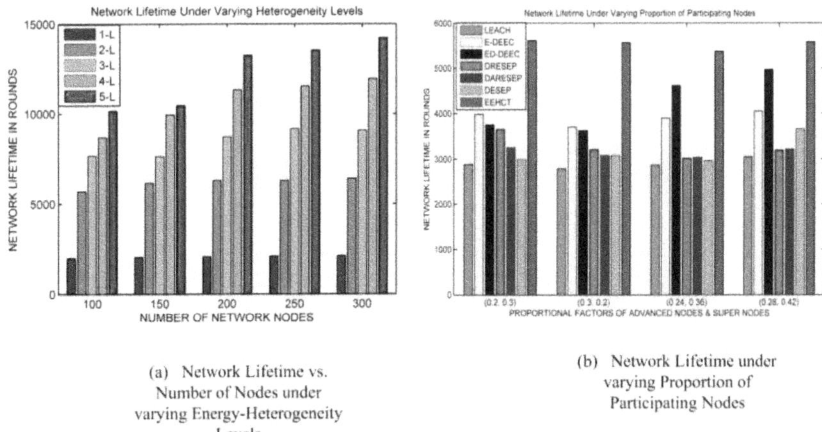

(a) Network Lifetime vs. Number of Nodes under varying Energy-Heterogeneity Levels

(b) Network Lifetime under varying Proportion of Participating Nodes

Fig. 2.10 Performance of EEHCT against the Peers with respect to Network Lifeitme [18]

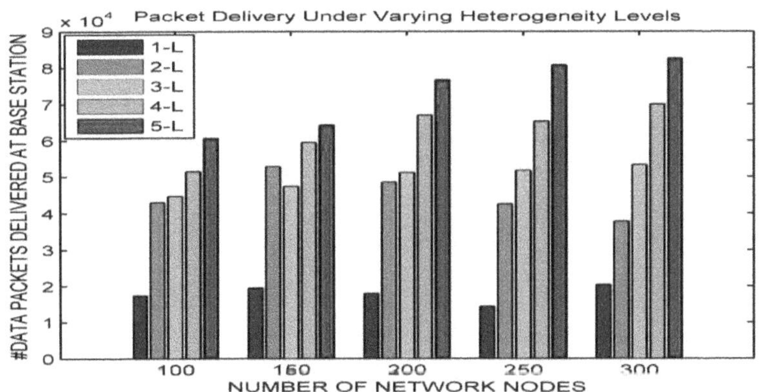

Fig. 2.11 Performance of EEHCT against the Peers with respect to Network Throughput [18]

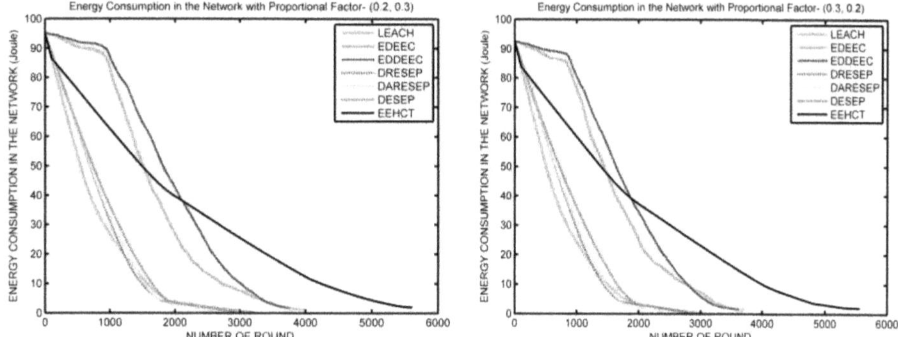

Fig. 2.12 Performance of EEHCT against the Peers with respect to
Energy Consumption [18]

Thus, the chapter elaborates multiple clustering strategies that
have been imparted by the researchers showcasing how the clustering
can be implemented heuristically in the network.

3. Metaheuristic Clustering in Wireless Sensor Network

As outlined in the previous chapter, a cluster-based architecture organizes network nodes into groups referred to as clusters based on certain criteria, such as node proximity, node degree, and residual energy. Once the nodes are organized into clusters, a selected node within each cluster acts as the cluster head (CH), which gathers data from all cluster members, combines it, and ultimately sends the aggregated data to the base station for further analysis or access by end-users. The cluster heads can transmit their data to the base station directly or utilize a multihop method, where each CH relays its data to another CH toward the base station. This localized organization and data aggregation, along with reduced communication overhead, enhance the overall lifespan of the network. It is evident from the discussion that various factors can be considered when forming clusters within the network, leading to the view of cluster formation as a multivariable optimization issue. To tackle this type of challenge, there are two commonly used methods: heuristic and metaheuristic techniques. The heuristic method is well-known for its tailored approach to a specific problem, utilizing the complete set of problem details to find an optimal solution. In contrast, the metaheuristic method employs a general approach to address complex, nonlinear multi-objective issues in real-world problems.

The current chapter explains how metaheuristic algorithms, such as differential evolution, have contributed to the development of load-balanced clusters that enable energy-efficient network operations.
It begins with a brief discussion on general metaheuristic algorithm and differential evolution and follows a discussion of notable clustering schemes created metaheuristically.

Metaheuristic Preliminaries and Related Concepts

The overall framework of the metaheuristic method is illustrated in Fig. 3.1. The approach begins with a randomly chosen group of solution vectors that progressively enhance throughout the iterations. After establishing the application-specific parameters like the scaling factor and crossover rate, the fitness of the existing solution set is assessed using a thoughtfully crafted fitness function. Then, the counter which keeps track of the iterations is initialized. Afterward, a selection from the population chosen is made, and the selected vectors undergo a variation phase (mutation/crossover).

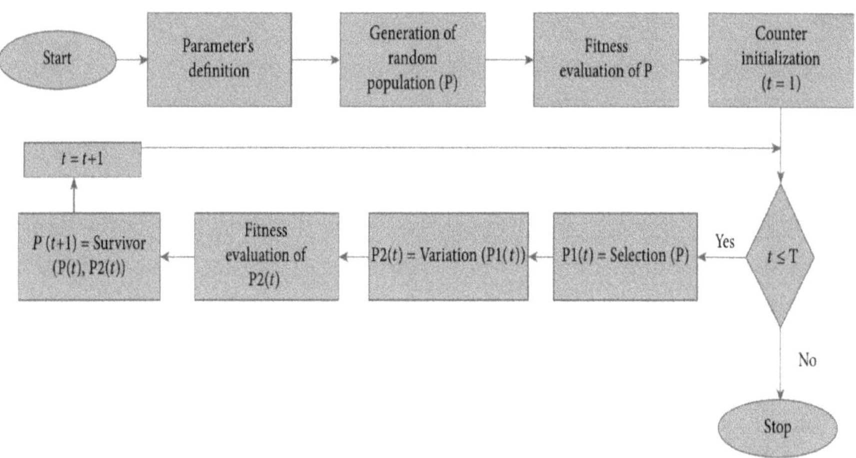

Figure 3.1 Metaheuristic Scheme- A Generic Approach

The updated vectors are evaluated again for their current fitness, and the population for the subsequent generation is determined through a survival function and a greedy selection strategy. The process of refining the solutions is repeated for a specified number of iterations, and ultimately, the most recent population is chosen as the final solution. A well-conceived and thoughtfully constructed fitness function is crucial for generating even better offspring in metaheuristic methods.

A diverse range of metaheuristic methods, including genetic algorithms (GA), genetic programming (GP), evolutionary programming (EP), evolution strategies (ES), differential evolution (DE), particle swarm optimization (PSO), ant colony optimization (ACO), and teaching-learning-based optimization (TLBO) can be found in the literature. Among this extensive collection of techniques, differential evolution has been widely embraced by researchers for clustering problems due to its ease of use and rapid convergence.

Differential Evolution- A Brief Introduction

In line with the overarching framework of metaheuristic techniques previously described, the process begins by establishing initial parameters, including the values for the scaling factor and crossover rate, along with a randomized collection of starting solutions (initial population) and the total number of iterations. In this context, each solution vector, referred to as a target vector, undergoes a mutation phase that is subsequently followed by a recombination phase. This sequence of mutation and recombination represents the variation phase illustrated in Fig. 3.1. Once the target vector completes the mutation phase, it is transformed into a donor or mutant vector. After the crossover or recombination phase, the donor vector is classified as the trial vector.

In the differential evolution framework, the next generation of solutions is produced only after all trial vectors have been created, unlike particle swarm optimization. The process of selecting which solutions advance to the next generation involves comparing pairs of target and trial vectors, occurring only after all target vectors have been converted into trial vectors. There are several mutation strategies available, as outlined in Table 3.1, including random, best, and target-to-best approaches. Furthermore, two types of crossover methods are applied: binomial and exponential crossovers.

Table 3.1 Differential Evolution Strategies [12]

DE scheme	Mutation strategy	Mutation expression	Crossover type
DE/rand/1/bin	Random	$V = X_{r_1} + F(X_{r_2} - X_{r_3})$	Binomial
DE/rand/2/exp	Random	$V = X_{r_1} + F(X_{r_2} - X_{r_3}) + F(X_{r_4} - X_{r_5})$	Exponential
DE/best/1/bin	Best	$V = X_{best} + F(X_{r_1} - X_{r_2})$	Binomial
DE/best/2/bin	Best	$V = X_{best} + F(X_{r_1} - X_{r_2}) + F(X_{r_3} - X_{r_4})$	Binomial
DE/target-to-best/1/exp	Target-to-best	$V = X_i + F(X_{best} - X_i) + F(X_{r_1} - X_{r_2})$	Exponential
DE/target-to-best/2/exp	Target-to-best	$V = X_i + F(X_{best} - X_i) + F(X_{r_1} - X_{r_2}) + F(X_{r_3} - X_{r_4})$	Exponential

Here, F refers to as mutation factor, V refers to the donor vector, and X_r is the rth target vector from the population.

The binomial and exponential crossover can be defined as follows:

Binomial Crossover:

$$u_i = \begin{cases} v_i & if\ r \le \rho_p\ or\ i = \delta \\ x_i & if\ r > \rho_p\ and\ i \ne \delta \end{cases} \tag{1}$$

where ρ_p is the crossover probability, δ is the randomly selected variable location from the set $\{1, 2, 3, \cdots k\}$, r is the random number between 0 and 1, u_i refers to the ith variable of the trial vector, v_i refers to the ith variable of donor/mutant vector, and x_i refers to the ith variable of the target vector. 'k' is the number of decision variable in a solution vector.

Exponential Crossover: In the exponential crossover, at very first, the nth variable from the donor vector is copied into the trial vector. Afterward, every subsequent variable from the donor vector is copied into the trial vector as long as the $r \le \rho_p$. Once $r > \rho_p$, variables from the target vector are copied into the trial vector.

As previously mentioned, the differential evolution (DE) approach consists of two primary steps: mutation and crossover. Table 3.1 outlines the key variations of mutation strategies and crossover methods that can be utilized based on the researcher's preferences to achieve optimized network solutions. In addition to the steps mentioned, having an appropriate fitness function to assess the effectiveness of the proposed solutions is essential for the success of the scheme. Therefore, the development of an objective-specific fitness function has also been emphasized in many solutions put forward by the research community. Numerous contributions have been made using this remarkable evolutionary technique of differential evolution to identify suitable clusters of nodes in wireless sensor networks (WSN). Here, some of the main schemes are presented and categorized based on the network's heterogeneity—Homogeneous and Heterogeneous.

Differential Evolution Based Clustering for Homogeneous WSN

The current subsection describes a scheme- Metaheuristic Load-Balancing-Based Clustering Technique (MLBCT) [12] which has been introduced as a clustering-based network solution for homogeneous wireless sensor network. In this reference, the network model detailed in chapter 1 is followed.

Metaheuristic Load-Balancing-Based Clustering Technique (MLBCT) in Wireless Sensor Networks
MLBCT is a scheme that relies on a base station (BS) to assist in establishing the necessary set of load-balanced clusters within the network. Utilizing a differential evolution-based approach, MLBCT begins with a phase known as bootstrapping, which aims to partition the network into a specific number of load-balanced clusters determined by user needs. To achieve this, it requires specific information about the nodes, including their unique identifiers and location details. The BS uses this data to identify the desired clusters that have evenly distributed loads through the application of differential evolution (DE). It determines the clusters along with their key roles, such as cluster heads and members. Subsequently, the BS notifies the chosen cluster heads about their roles and the members assigned to them. Once the cluster heads are informed by the base station, they prepare and disseminate the TDMA schedules to their respective cluster members.

The network's operation is structured into rounds, with each round consisting of a steady-state phase followed by a responsible node selection phase. In a manner similar to the traditional steady-state phase, member nodes send their measurements to their designated cluster heads, who then aggregate the data and forward it to the base station. Following this, the responsible node selection phase occurs, during which the current cluster heads randomly choose a node from their clusters to act as the cluster head for the upcoming round and communicate this information to their members.

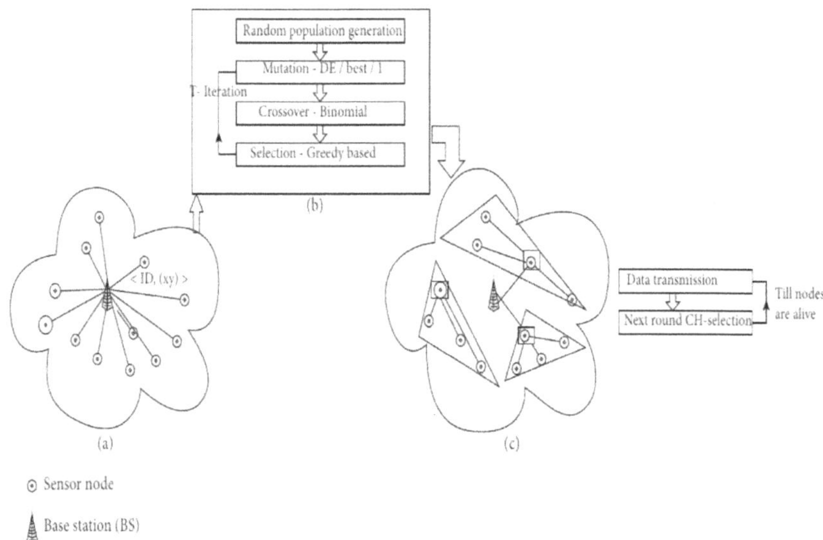

Figure 3.2 Working of MLBCT [12]

Bootstrapping:

Bootstrapping is designed for creating clusters in the network that are well-balanced in terms of load. The base station spearheads this stage and executes network partitioning using differential evolution. Initially, the base station requests the nodes within the network to share their specific details, such as ID, energy level, and locations. The base station utilizes this data to determine how to form clusters by implementing the differential evolution (DE) scheme.

As described in the section 3.1 and under Fig. 3.1, the very first step is to create set of initial population as follows:

MLBCT provides a finite set of population vectors, all of which have a length of N. In this scenario, a network consisting of N sensor nodes is divided into k clusters, with k being predetermined. Each population vector denotes how each node is allocated to a randomly selected cluster head. The initial collection of populations is generated randomly in the following manner:

If $\Lambda_{i,G}$ refers to the ith vector of the Gth generation (also known as target vectors), then:

$$\Lambda_{i,G} = [\lambda_{1,i,G}, \lambda_{2,i,G}, \lambda_{3,i,G}, ..., \lambda_{N,i,G}] \tag{2}$$

Where, $\lambda_{1,i,G}, \lambda_{2,i,G}, \lambda_{3,i,G}, ..., \lambda_{N,i,G}$ refer to the numbers chosen randomly between 0 and 1 with $\lambda_{j,i,G}$ indicating assignment of s_j node to one of k cluster heads.

In this process of deciding clusters, MLBCT implements the following fitness function, (2), to evaluate its population.

$$\Phi_{ff} = \frac{1}{\sqrt{1/k * \sum_{l=1}^{k}(AvCenergy - Cluster^{l}_{ResEnergy})^2} * \sqrt{1/k * \sum_{l=1}^{k}(AvCsize - Csize_l)^2} * \sum_{l=1}^{k} dist_l(i,j)}$$

$$\tag{3}$$

where *AvCenergy* refers to the average clusters' energy and *Cluster$^l_{ResEnergy}$* is the lth cluster's energy; *AvCsize* is the average size of the clusters formed and C_{size_l} is the size of lth cluster. '*k*' is priori known number of clusters. MLBCT employs DE/best/1/bin to enhance its population through mutation, succeeded by a binomial crossover stage.

Once the base station finishes the network partitioning process, it alerts the cluster heads about their status and the corresponding member nodes. Subsequently, the network activities are segmented into rounds, which include the steady-state and responsible node selection stages.

Steady-State Phase:

This phase is dedicated to data transmission, wherein the cluster members send data to their respective cluster heads. Cluster heads then aggregate and forward the received data to the base station.

Responsible Node Selection Phase

At the end of the steady-state phase, the cluster heads within their clusters randomly select a node to serve as the heads for the subsequent rounds. This decision is communicated to the members by the head and acknowledged by the members.

The MLBCT scheme shows superior performance compared to peer models such as the Improved Differential Evolution-based LEACH (ImDE-LEACH) [25], the Differential Evolution Based Clustering Routing Protocol (DEBCRP) [26], and the LEACH protocol [9], particularly regarding network lifespan, throughput, and energy efficiency, as illustrated in the self-explanatory figures—Fig. 3.3, 3.4, 3.5, and 3.6.

To strengthen this assertion, the authors evaluated MLBCT's performance across various network setups. Two distinct configurations, referred to as WSN#1 and WSN#2, were analyzed. WSN#1 outlines a 100 x 100 m² network with the base station situated at the center, specifically at (50m, 50m). In contrast, WSN#2 places the base station outside the sensing area, precisely at (50m, 150m). Both WSN#1 and WSN#2 assessed the effectiveness of MLBCT, DEBCRP, ImDE-LEACH, and LEACH under varying node densities, including scenarios with 50, 100, 150, and 200 nodes. Figures 3.3 and 3.4 illustrate MLBCT's advantage in network lifetime, measured by the instances of the first and last nodes' deaths within both WSN#1 and WSN#2 configurations. In both scenarios, MLBCT surpasses all other methodologies.

Similarly, Fig. 3.5 and 3.6 showcase the MLBCT's supremacy in terms of throughout and average energy consumption

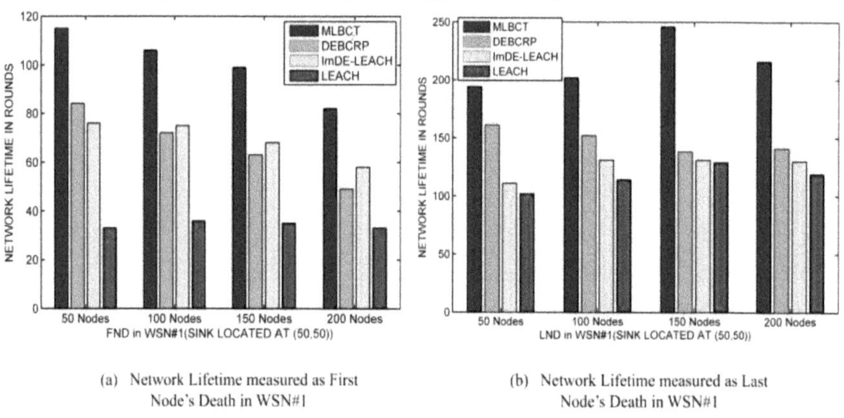

(a) Network Lifetime measured as First Node's Death in WSN#1

(b) Network Lifetime measured as Last Node's Death in WSN#1

Figure 3.3 Network Lifetime measured as First and Last Node's Death in WSN#1 [12]

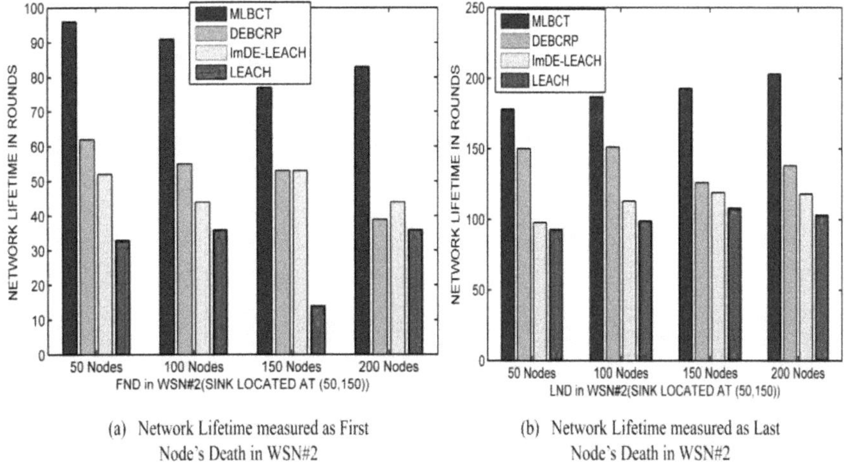

(a) Network Lifetime measured as First
Node's Death in WSN#2

(b) Network Lifetime measured as Last
Node's Death in WSN#2

Figure 3.4 Network Lifetime measured as First and Last Node's Death in
WSN#2 [12]

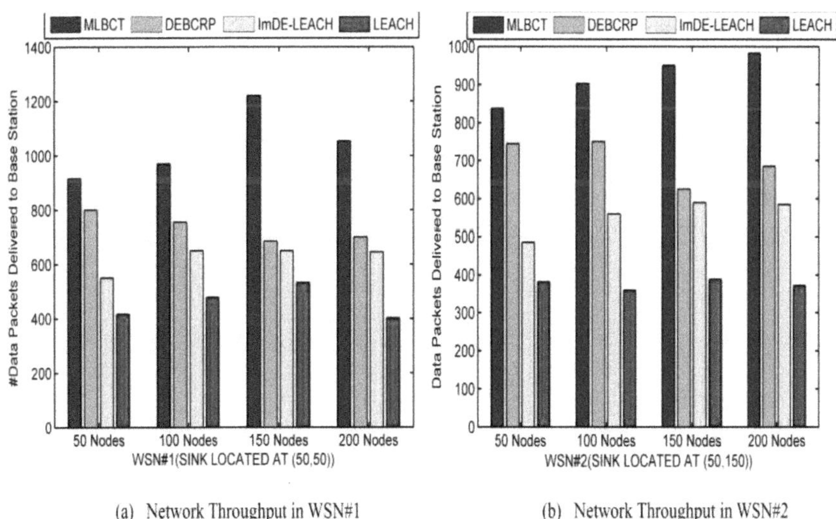

(a) Network Throughput in WSN#1

(b) Network Throughput in WSN#2

Figure 3.5 Network Throughput measured as Data Packets Delivered to
Base Station [12]

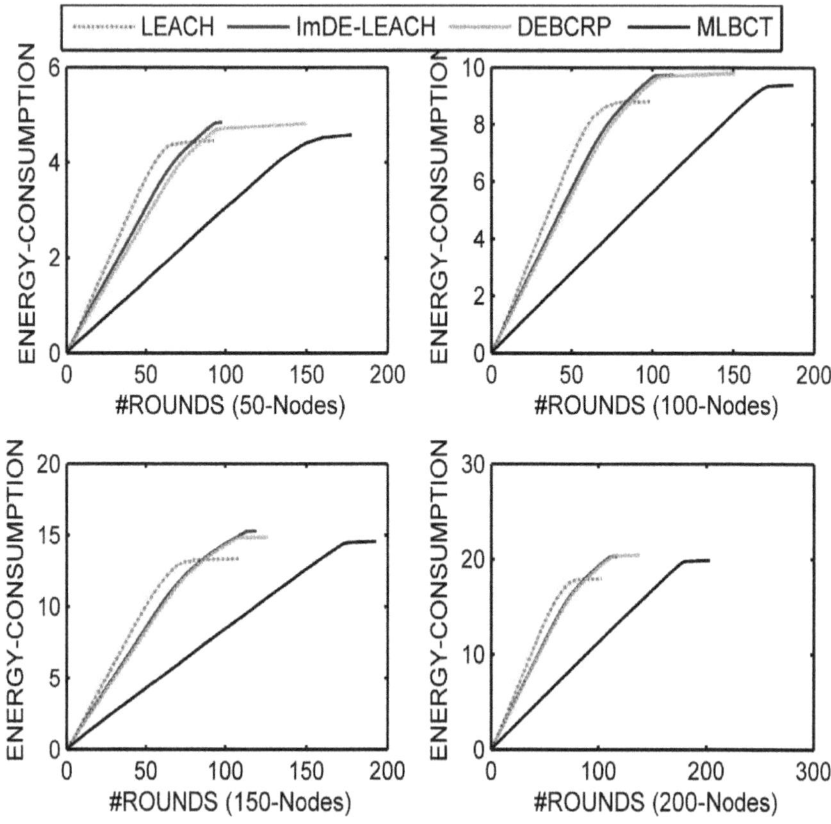

Figure 3.6 Network Energy Consumption under varying Node-Density [12]

Differential Evolution Based Clustering for Heterogeneous WSNs

This section introduces two well-known methodologies—DEICA[1] and MMHCT [13]—that demonstrate how the Differential Evolution metaheuristic approach can aid in establishing load-balanced clusters, promoting energy-efficient network operations.

a) **A Differential Evolution-based Improved Clustering Algorithm (DEICA) for IoT-based heterogeneous wireless sensor networks**:

A Differential Evolution-based Improved Clustering Algorithm (DEICA) [1] is a metaheuristic solution focused on clustering for two-tier wireless sensor networks. A two-tier wireless sensor network consists of two types of nodes: a limited number of energy-rich sensor nodes and a larger group of standard nodes. The high-energy nodes, referred to as control nodes, are designed to manage all tasks that require significant energy. DEICA is a clustering-centric approach that establishes clusters solely around these high-energy control nodes.

These control nodes are designated to serve as the cluster heads. Consequently, they are responsible for collecting data from their associated members, aggregating the gathered information, and sending the compiled data to a remote base station for further access by end users. The normal nodes are tasked with sensing environmental conditions and communicating with their respective cluster heads (control nodes).

Shortly after the deployment of the nodes, the base station divides the network into suitable clusters centered on the control nodes using a differential evolution-based method. The partitioning of the network is a crucial process in a clustering-oriented network solution, as careful execution can lead to enhanced network performance. This is why DEICA takes into account several factors, such as the proximity of nodes, the population density, the energy levels of potential clusters, and the longevity of control nodes when forming clusters.

Once the network has been successfully partitioned into well-balanced clusters using differential evolution as the foundational metaheuristic strategy, the data transmission stage commences. In this phase, the member nodes will continuously send data to their respective cluster heads in each subsequent round. The specifics of the method are outlined below. Since this is a base station (BS) assisted scheme, the BS segments the network into a limited number of appropriate clusters. Similar to its previous approaches like [12,13], the BS assigns the responsibility for subsequent network operations to the nodes right after the clusters are formed.

The network operations consist of the setup and the data transmission phases. The initialization stage is performed only once initially, unlike the data transmission stage, which takes place repeatedly in each successive round. This initialization stage includes three sub-stages: bootstrapping, clustering, and local improvement. During the bootstrapping sub-stage, the standard sensor nodes transmit their unique identity numbers (UINs) so that control nodes within their communication range can receive them. The control nodes (CNs) create a record of the nodes within their communication range and send this information to the BS to establish load-balanced clusters. Afterward, the base station triggers the clustering sub-phase. Using the information obtained from the control nodes, the base station forms the clusters during this sub-phase. The base station employs the differential evolution strategy to create clusters according to the specifics outlined in the following subsections.

The clusters that have been established so far are further enhanced through a local improvement phase aimed at achieving a better balance among the clusters. This local improvement phase refines the clusters by exchanging nodes within them as needed to ensure an even distribution in node count. Once this local improvement sub-phase concludes and the clusters are finalized, the base station notifies the control nodes of their roles and the corresponding member sensor nodes. The control nodes then reach out to the member sensor nodes and share their specific TDMA schedules for data transmission. The current clustering sub-phase wraps up with the delivery of TDMA schedules to the sensor nodes. Following this, the data transmission phase is activated, during which the sensor nodes send their readings to the designated control node, which then consolidates the information received and relays it to the base station.

In accordance with the conventional differential evolution (DE) methodology, DEICA consists of phases for generating a random population, mutation, crossover, and selection. The selection phase includes a comparison of the population vectors and their mutated counterparts based on fitness values. Figure 3.7 illustrates the comprehensive scheme of the DEICA.

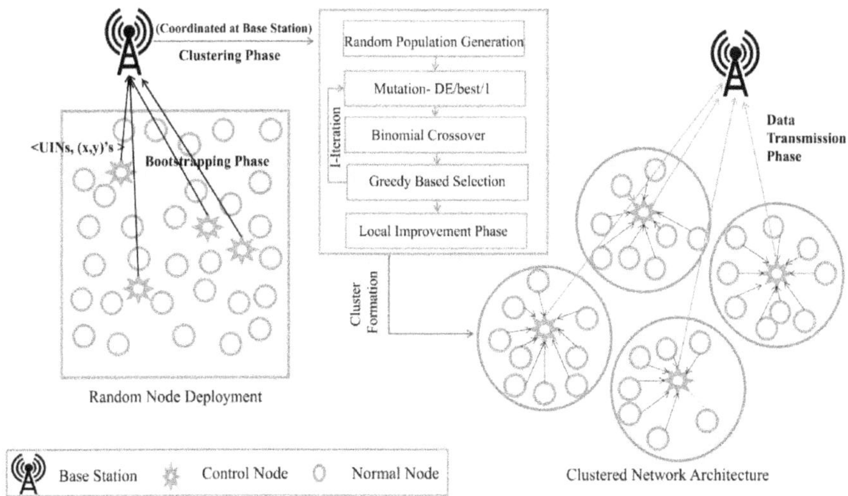

Figure 3.7 Network Operations in DEICA

The initial population is created similarly to the method used in MLBCT, with the distinction that DEICA designates the control nodes as the cluster heads. Consequently, each population vector assigns the normal nodes to one of the designated control nodes. Once the population is generated, an appropriate fitness function has been established as detailed in [13] according to (4).

$$\Phi_{ff} = \frac{C_{ACEnergy} * C_{ANDegree}}{\sigma_{LifeCN} * \sigma_{ADistCN} * \sigma_{IdealCSize} * \sigma_{ACEnergy}}$$

(4)

where $C_{ACEnergy}$ is the cumulative average cluster energy, $C_{ANDegree}$ is the cumulative average node degree, σ_{LifeCN} is the standard deviation of the lifetime of the control nodes, $\sigma_{ADistCN}$ is the standard deviation of the average cluster distance, $\sigma_{IdealCSize}$ be the standard deviation of the ideal size of a cluster, and $\sigma_{ACEnergy}$ is the standard deviation of the average cluster energy.

DEICA implements DE/best/1/bin for the refinement of its population through the mutation, followed by binomial crossover phase.

After determining the optimal population vector, DEICA implements an additional phase for local improvement to refine the obtained clusters. In this local enhancement phase, the base station assesses the sizes of the existing clusters against the ideal size (calculated by dividing the total number of nodes by the number of control nodes). If a cluster's size exceeds the ideal size, the surplus nodes are allocated randomly to nearby suitable clusters. The suitability for reallocating nodes to these clusters is based on two criteria: the size of the target cluster must be smaller than the ideal size, and the control node of the destination cluster should be at the minimum distance from all available control nodes. This procedure is performed successively for each resultant cluster created.

During the data transmission phase, the cluster members transmit their data to their designated control nodes. The control nodes then collect and send the compiled data to the base station. To demonstrate its superiority over other methods in terms of network longevity, energy usage, and throughput, the authors carried out various simulations under different network configurations as shown in Figures 3.8 to 3.10.

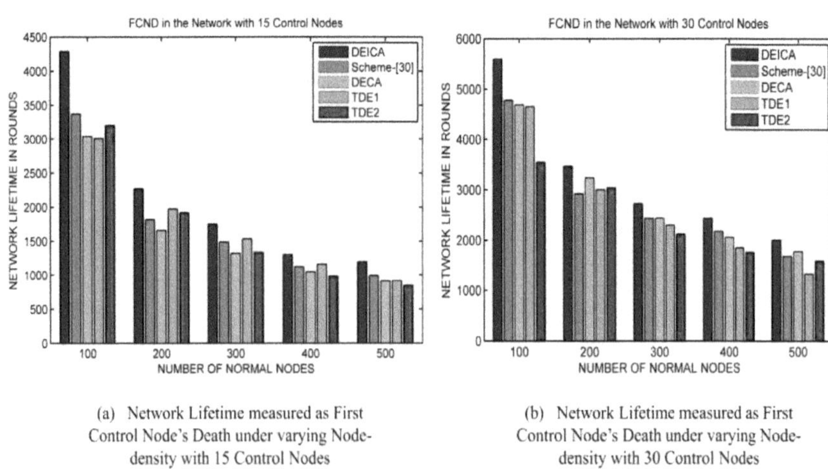

(a) Network Lifetime measured as First Control Node's Death under varying Node-density with 15 Control Nodes

(b) Network Lifetime measured as First Control Node's Death under varying Node-density with 30 Control Nodes

Figure 3.8 Network Lifetime under varying Network Configuration [1]

Network lifetime has been defined as the death of the first control node in this performance comparison and the outperformance of DEICA over its peers is evident in Fig. 3.8 in both the network configurations i.e. with 15 and 30 control nodes respectively.

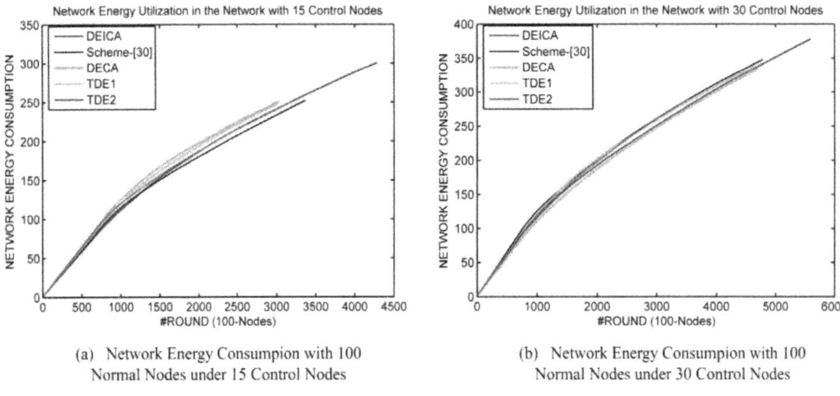

(a) Network Energy Consumpion with 100 Normal Nodes under 15 Control Nodes

(b) Network Energy Consumpion with 100 Normal Nodes under 30 Control Nodes

Figure 3.9 Network Energy Consumption under varying Network Configuration [1]

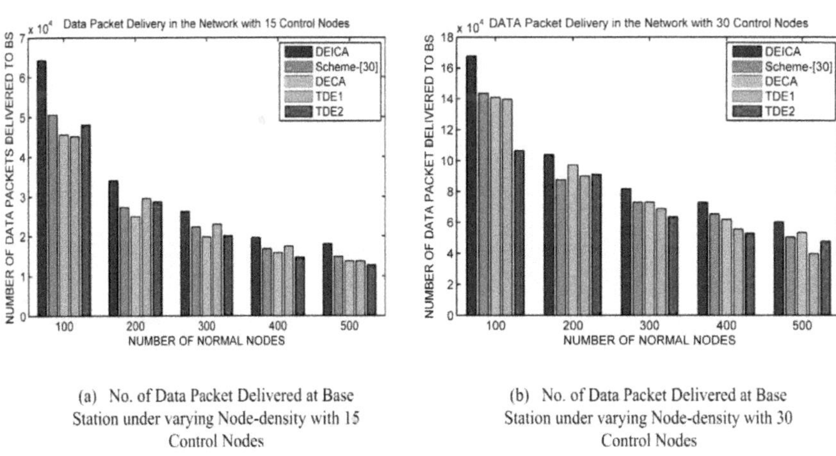

(a) No. of Data Packet Delivered at Base Station under varying Node-density with 15 Control Nodes

(b) No. of Data Packet Delivered at Base Station under varying Node-density with 30 Control Nodes

Figure 3.10 Network Throughput under varying Network Configuration [1]

b) Metaheuristic Multilevel Heterogeneous Clustering Technique (MMHCT) for Heterogeneous Wireless Sensor Networks:

MMHCT is designed to divide an n ($\geq$ 1)-level Heterogeneous Wireless Sensor Network (HWSN) into a limited number of energy-balanced clusters made up of sensor nodes that are as close together as possible. The phrase energy-balanced clusters signifies the creation of clusters with roughly equal energy levels. Additionally, organizing the nodes with minimal distance between them lowers the cost of communication within the cluster. Through the use of differential evolution, MMHCT effectively segments the network into energy-balanced clusters where the nodes are near one another. MMHCT operates with the assistance of a base station, which determines the clusters based on a fitness function that prioritizes the energy levels of the clusters and the distances among the nodes within each cluster. After the base station establishes the clusters, it delegates the responsibilities for network operations to the network nodes by notifying the selected cluster heads for the initial time. The specifics of the scheme are outlined below.

MMHCT organizes the network operations into distinct rounds. Each round consists of three phases: clustering, steady-state, and responsible node selection. The clustering phase occurs only once and is designed to create clusters by the base station. In determining how to partition the network, the base station utilizes a fitness function that takes into account the spatial distribution of the nodes along with their energy levels. After establishing energy-balanced clusters and choosing suitable cluster heads, the base station notifies the selected cluster heads about their duties and responsibilities, as well as their corresponding members. Following this, the cluster heads assume the responsibilities of the network and manage these in two repeated phases: steady-state and responsible node selection.

Clustering Phase:

The base station carries out the clustering phase as described in [12]. Initially, during the network operation, the base station requests that each node provide its data, including identity, energy status, and location details. The base station analyzes this information from the contributing nodes and performs cluster formation in the network using differential evolution techniques.

Since, MMHCT attempts to partition the network into a finite number of clusters of approximately equal energy, standard deviation of the cluster's energy ($\sigma_{CEnergy}$) along with the nodes' proximity have been taken into consideration as the main parameters in deciding the fitness functions as follows:

$$\Phi_{ff} = \frac{1}{\sqrt{1/k * \sum_{i=1}^{k}(AvgCEnergy - Cluster_{ResEnergy}^{i})^2}} * \frac{1}{\sum_{m=1}^{k} Distance_m(i,j)}$$

$$(4)$$

where *AvgCEnenrgy* is the average cluster energy, *Cluster$_{ResEnergy}^{i}$* denotes the residual energy of the ith cluster, k refers to the number of clusters, and *Distance$_m$(i, j)* is the collective distance between any two nodes in mth cluster.

Similar to MLBCT, MMHCT also incorporates DE/best/1 and a binomial crossover as its mutation and crossover methods during the clustering process. After the base station successfully generates all trial vectors, it selects the next generation of the population by implementing a greedy selection from both the current population and the trial vectors. Consequently, the base station identifies the energy-balanced clusters along with their corresponding cluster heads. It then communicates the responsibilities and cluster members to the designated cluster heads. The chosen cluster heads subsequently devise and share a TDMA schedule for their clusters with the respective members.

Steady-State Phase:

This phase is designed to gather information and relay it to the base station. At the start of each new round, cluster members monitor their environment and send their readings to the cluster head. The cluster head then consolidates the incoming data packets and transmits the normalized version to the base station on behalf of its cluster.

Responsible Node Selection Phase:

After the heads in the steady-state phase relay the clusters' information to the base station, the CHs choose a random node within their clusters to serve as the heads for the upcoming round. They inform their respective cluster members about the details of the chosen cluster heads.

To showcase its supremacy over the peers like DEBCRP [26] and LEACH [9] in terms of network lifetime, energy consumption, and throughput, authors have conducted various simulation under varying levels of energy heterogeneity as demonstrated in Fig. 3.11 - Fig. 3.13.

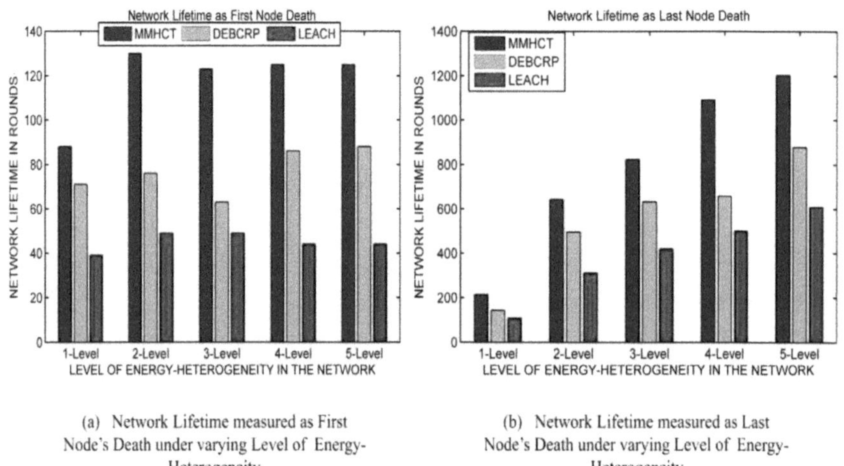

(a) Network Lifetime measured as First Node's Death under varying Level of Energy-Heterogeneity

(b) Network Lifetime measured as Last Node's Death under varying Level of Energy-Heterogeneity

Figure 3.11 Network Lifetime measured as Death of the First and Last Node [13]

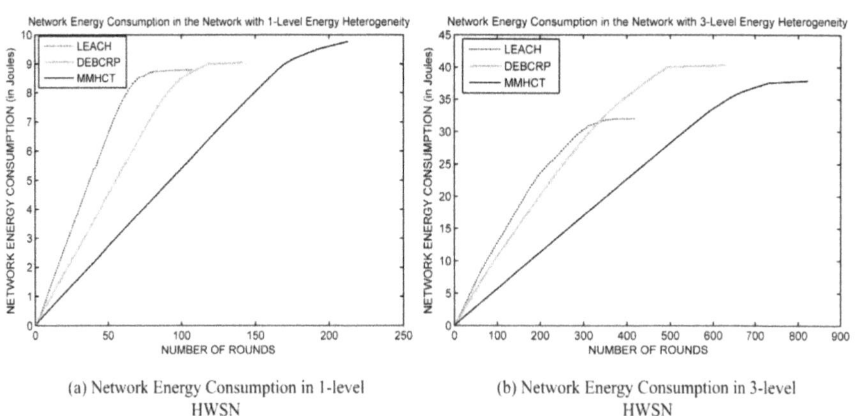

(a) Network Energy Consumption in 1-level HWSN

(b) Network Energy Consumption in 3-level HWSN

Figure 3.12 Network Energy Consumption over Rounds [13]

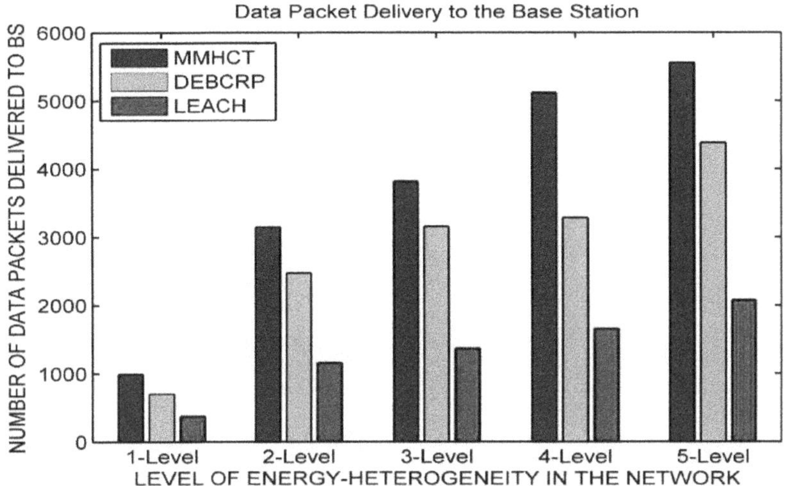

Figure 3.13 No. Of Data Packet Received at Base Station under varying Levels of Heterogeneity [13]

From the above figures, the supremacy of MMHCT is evident over its peers in varying network configurations/energy-heterogeneity levels.

4. Open Issues and Research Directions

The previous chapters have highlighted that enhancing energy efficiency in resource-constrained wireless sensor networks (WSNs) presents a significant challenge for researchers. Over the years, clustering has emerged as a crucial strategy in the development of energy-efficient network operations. As computational technology has advanced, the implementation of metaheuristic algorithms has become increasingly feasible, allowing researchers to innovate in this area. Consequently, clustering solutions that employ metaheuristic techniques have risen to become a preferred approach among many in the research community.

Challenges and Issues

a) **Mobility of the nodes**

Since the inception of wireless sensor networks, addressing mobility has been considered a major challenge. There are essentially two types of mobility in these networks: node mobility and sink mobility. Node mobility pertains to the movement of sensor nodes, which can change their positions based on the application's requirements; on the other hand, sink mobility typically refers to the independent movement of sink node(s), particularly to gather data directly from the nodes distributed throughout the network. Whether it involves node mobility or sink mobility, it must be managed with care, as the movement of nodes or sinks can lead to significant topological changes in the network.

b) **Heterogeneity of the nodes**

In the modern era, the implementation of wireless sensor networks requires the combination of various types of diverse sensors designed for specific uses, such as monitoring wildlife and environmental tracking.

This diversity, marked by nodes that have unique abilities and functions, can result in a variety of intricate technical issues. These issues may stem from the necessity to efficiently manage and coordinate sensors that utilize different communication protocols, possess varying data processing capabilities, and have different levels of power consumption, all of which are essential for the effective functioning of sensor networks in a range of environments.

c) **Load distribution**

Sensors, which are often limited by their power supply, can experience a significant challenge known as energy depletion. When this occurs, the affected nodes are unable to contribute to ongoing network operations, leading to potential failures in the system. To mitigate the risk of premature node failures, it is crucial to implement strategies that ensure the workload is distributed evenly across all nodes. This balanced distribution helps to prolong the operational life of each node and maintain the overall efficiency and reliability of the network.

d) **Scalability**

Scalability is a crucial aspect to consider when addressing the challenges of clustering. It is essential to ensure that any proposed clustering solution can effectively handle varying amounts of data without a decline in performance or accuracy. A scalable clustering approach should be able to accommodate larger datasets or increased complexity while maintaining its efficiency and reliability.

e) **Intracluster and inter-cluster communication**

Intra-cluster communication involves the exchange of data between the various members and the head node within a cluster, while inter-cluster communication pertains to the interactions among the heads of different clusters. The process of forming a cluster must effectively address the reduction of the mentioned costs.

f) **Cluster formation**

The success of any clustering scheme relies heavily on several important parameters that are specific to each cluster. These parameters include the number of clusters, their respective sizes, and other related factors that play a vital role in determining the overall effectiveness and efficiency of the approach. Understanding and optimizing these cluster-specific characteristics is essential for achieving the desired outcomes.

g) **Cluster head selection**

In the clustering process, a comprehensive evaluation of various parameters is vital for achieving optimal performance. Important factors to examine include the proximity of nodes to each other, which impacts the efficiency of communication; the degree of each node, reflecting its connections and influence within the network; and the remaining energy of the nodes, which dictates their capability to engage in data transmission and processing over time. Considering these aspects will enhance the effectiveness and sustainability of a clustering strategy.

h) **Coverage & connectivity**

The coverage in Wireless Sensor Networks (WSN) can be categorized into three types based on how sensors monitor the events within the sensing area: area coverage, target coverage, and barrier coverage. Area coverage involves overseeing a designated region of interest, while target coverage focuses on monitoring a specific set of targets rather than the broader area. Barrier coverage is aimed at surveying a perimeter, particularly for detecting intrusions. Connectivity pertains to the degree to which the nodes in the area can interact with one another. Proper attention to both of these aspects-coverage and connectivity- is crucial for developing an effective network solution. Different applications may necessitate network arrangements with varying levels of connectivity and coverage.

Future Research Directions

- Metaheuristic methods can be utilized to efficiently address critical issues in transforming current simulation scenarios into practical real-world applications using cross-layer optimization.

● The emphasis on the quality of clusters, particularly regarding load-balancing, can be explored in greater detail since it significantly influences the effectiveness of the clustering process.

● Investigating the concept of deploying multiple mobile sinks could enhance energy efficiency while mitigating energy holes within the network.

● Further optimization of the frequency at which cluster heads rotate could lead to improvements in the overall lifespan of the network.

● Addressing security concerns at the node level can further enhance routing protocols.

● Integrating optimization techniques with machine learning approaches can significantly enhance the clustering process and overall network performance.

● A well-balanced combination of various metaheuristic methodologies, such as genetic algorithms, differential evolution, swarm intelligence techniques, and teaching-learning based optimization, could be pursued to enhance network longevity and user experience.

● Proper attention to different factors like node proximity, node degree, node location, node residual energy, and node mobility can be given to optimize the overall clustering process for determining quality clusters.

● The effects of the physical and data link layers on the clustering process can be examined and fine-tuned using optimization techniques.

REFERENCE

[1] Chaurasiya SK, Biswas A, Nayyar A, Zaman Jhanjhi N, Banerjee R. DEICA: A differential evolution-based improved clustering algorithm for IoT-based heterogeneous wireless sensor networks. Int J Commun Syst. 2023;e5420. doi:10.1002/dac.5420

[2] Ying Li, and Radim Bartos, A survey of protocols for Intermittently Connected Delay-Tolerant Wireless Sensor Networks, Journal of Network and Computer Applications 41 (2014) 411–423, DOI: http://dx.doi.org/10.1016/j.jnca.2013.10.003

[3] Dumka, A., Chaurasiya, S. K., Biswas, A., and Mandoria, H. L, A Complete Guide to Wireless Sensor Networks: from Inception to Current Trends, 1st Edition; CRC Press, Boca Raton, Florida, USA, 2019, ISBN 9781032401416.10.1109/TNSM.2020.3035315.

[4] I. F. Akyildiz, Weilian Su, Yogesh Sankarasubramaniam, and Erdal Cayirci, A Survey on Sensor Networks, IEEE Communication Magazine 40(8) 2002, pp. 393-422, DOI: https://doi.org/10.1109/MCOM.2002.1024422.

[5] Soheil Ghiasi, Ankur Srivastava, Xiaojian Yang, and Majid Sarrafzadeh, Optimal Energy Aware Clustering in Sensor Networks, SENSORS Journal, Vol. 2, No. 7, 2002, pp. 258-269, DOI: https://doi.org/10.3390/s20700258.

[6] M.Mehdi Afsar, Mohammad-H. Tayarani-N: Clustering in Sensor Networks: A Literature Survey. Journal of Network and Computer Applications 46 (2014), pp. 198-226.

[7] Sandip Kumar Chaurasiya, Tumpa Pal, Sipra Das Bit, An Enhanced Energy Efficient Protocol with Static Clustering for WSN, Proceedings IEEE Xplore, Int'l Conf. of Information Networking (ICOIN), Kuala Lumpur, Malaysia, March 2011, pp. 58-63, DOI: 10.1109/ICOIN.2011.5723134.

[8] Sandip K Chaurasiya, Jaydeep Sen, Srirupa Chatterjee, and Sipra Das Bit, EBLEC: An Energy-Balanced Lifetime Enhancing Clustering for WSN, Proceeding IEEE Xplore, 14th Int'l Conf. on Advanced Communication \& Technology-2012, PyeongChang, Korea (South), Feb. 2012, pp. 189-194, INSPEC Accession Number: 12656578.

[9] W. R. Heinzelman, A. Chandrakasan, and H. Balkrishnan, Energy-Efficient Communication Protocol for Wireless Microsensor Networks, in Proceedings of 33rd Hawaii International Conference on System Science, Vol. 2, Jan. 2000, pp.1-10, DOI: 10.1109/HICSS.2000.926982.

[10] W. R. Heinzelman A. Chandrakasan, and H.Balkrishnan, An application -Specific Protocol Architecture for Wireless Microsensor Networks, IEEE Trans. Wireless Communication, Vol. 1, No. 4, Oct. 2002, pp. 660-670, DOI: 10.1109/TWC.2002.804190.

[11] Sandip K Chaurasiya, Joydeep Mondal, Suman Datta, Field-of-View based hierarchical clustering to prolong network lifetime of WMSN with obstacles, Proceeding IEEE Xplore, Int'l Conf. on Electronics, Communication, and Computational Engineering, Chennai, INDIA, Nov. 2014, pp.72-77, DOI: 10.1109/ICECCE.2014.7086638.

[12] Sandip K Chaurasiya, Arindam Biswas, Prasit Kumar Bandyopadhyay, Amit Banerjee, and Rajib Banerjee, "Metaheuristic Load- Balancing Based Clustering Technique for Wireless Sensor Networks, Hindawi, Wireless Communication and Mobile Computing, Volume 2022, Article ID 8911651, 21 pages, https://doi.org/10.1155/2022/8911651.

[13] S. K. Chaurasiya, A. Biswas and R. Banerjee, "Metaheuristic Multilevel Heterogeneous Clustering Technique for Heterogeneous Wireless Sensor Networks", 2021 10th International Conference on Internet of Everything, Microwave Engineering, Communication and Networks (IEMECON), 2021, pp. 1-6, doi: 10.1109/IEMECON53809.2021.9689098.

[14] O. Younis and S. Fahmy, HEED: A Hybrid Energy-Efficient Distributed Clustering Approach for Ad hoc Sensor Networks, IEEE

Transaction on Mobile Computing, Vol. 3, No. 4, 2004, pp. 660-669, DOI: 10.1109/TMC.2004.41.

[15] A.S. Zahmati, B.Abolhassani, Ali A.B.Shirazi, and A.S. Bahitiari, "An Energy-Efficient Protocol with Static Clustering for Wireless Sensor Networks", International Journal of Electronics, Circuit, and Systems Vol. 1, No. 2, May. 2007, pp. 135-138.

[16] N. Javaid, T. N. Qureshi, A.H. Khan, A. Iqbal, E. Akhtar, M. Ishfaq, EDDEEC: Enhanced Developed Distributed Energy-Efficient Clustering for Heterogeneous Wireless Sensor Networks, Procedia Computer Science 19 (2013) 914 – 919, DOI: https://doi.org/10.1016/j.procs.2013.06.125.

[17] Chaurasiya, S.K., Biswas, A., Bandyopadhyay, P.K. (2023). Heterogeneous Energy-Efficient Clustering Protocol for Wireless Sensor Networks. In: Mishra, B., Tiwari, M. (eds) VLSI, Microwave and Wireless Technologies. Lecture Notes in Electrical Engineering, vol 877. Springer, Singapore. https://doi.org/10.1007/978-981-19-0312-0_16.

[18] S.K.Chaurasiya, S. Mondal, A. Biswas, A. Nayyar, M.A. Shah, and R. Banerjee, "An Energy-Efficient Hybrid Clustering Technique (EEHCT) for IoT-based Multilevel Heterogeneous Wireless Sensor Networks," in IEEE Access, vol. -, pp. --, 2023, doi: 10.1109/ACCESS.2023.

[19] L. Qing, Q. Zhu, M. Wang, Design of a distributed energy-efficient clustering algorithm for heterogeneous wireless sensor networks. ELSEVIER, Computer Communications 29, 2006, pp 2230- 2237, DOI: https://doi.org/10.1016/j.comcom.2006.02.017.

[20] Elbhiri, B. , Saadane, R. , El Fkihi, S. , Aboutajdine, D., Developed Distributed Energy-Efficient Clustering (DDEEC) for heterogeneous wireless sensor networks, in: 5th International Symposium on IV Communications and Mobile Network (ISVC), 2010, DOI: 10.1109/ISVC.2010.5656252.

[21] Parul Saini, Ajay. K. Sharma, E-DEEC- Enhanced Distributed Energy Efficient Clustering Scheme for heterogeneous WSN, in: 2010

1st International Conference on Parallel, Distributed and Grid Computing (PDGC - 2010), pp. 205-210, DOI: 10.1109/PDGC.2010.5679898.

[22] A. Naeem, A. R. Javed, M. Rizwan, S. Abbas, J. C. -W. Lin and T. R. Gadekallu, "DARE-SEP: A Hybrid Approach of Distance Aware Residual Energy-Efficient SEP for WSN," in IEEE Transactions on Green Communications and Networking, vol. 5, no. 2, pp. 611-621, June 2021, doi: 10.1109/TGCN.2021.3067885

[23] A. Hossan and P. K. Choudhury, "DE-SEP: Distance and Energy Aware Stable Election Routing Protocol for Heterogeneous Wireless Sensor Network," in IEEE Access, vol. 10, pp. 55726-55738, 2022, doi: 10.1109/ACCESS.2022.3177190.

[24] Mittal, N., Singh, U., "Distance-Based Residual Energy-Efficient Stable Election Protocol for WSNs," Arab J Sci Eng 40, 1637–1646 (2015), https://doi.org/10.1007/s13369-015-1641-x

[25] X. Li et al., A Differential Evolution based Routing Algorithm for Envirnomental Monitoring Wireless Sensor Networks, Sensors, vol. 10, no. 6, 2010, pp. 5425-5442.

[26] Kaddi M, Khalili Z, and Bouchra M, A Differential Evolution Based Clustering and Routing Protocol for WSN, 2020 International Conference on Mathematics and Information Technology, Adrar, Ageria, Feb. 18-19, 2020, pp. 190-195.

* 9 7 9 8 8 9 6 7 3 5 5 0 2 *